Gaslighting Games

*The Manipulative Power to Play with
People's Minds and Control Them for Life*

Emory Green

CLAIM YOUR FREE GIFT

This book comes with a free bonus item.

Head straight to the last chapter to quickly claim your gift today!

TABLE OF CONTENTS

INTRODUCTION

We are all driven by desires and wants and we all have an innate need to control certain aspects of our lives and those of the people around us. We want people to love us a certain way, talk to us in a particular manner, and treat us with respect. And there is absolutely nothing wrong with that. But what if, hypothetically speaking, you or the other person in the relationship is always controlling the outcome of your interactions by being manipulative and using words and actions that push the other party to respond in a manner that is only beneficial to them? Does that make them just selfish or are they gaslighters?

In this book, I will expose the difference between the selfish, naturally manipulative tendencies of narcissism and gaslighting. Gaslighting is a very specific form of manipulation that any one of us can fall into, either as the perpetrator or the victim. Not only will I define what gaslighting is, I will also give real-life examples of gaslighting and how it occurs in various aspects of our lives. Reading this book will help you be able to identify the different techniques and tactics used by gaslighters or begin to notice them in your behavior if you are one. Our love for others and our opinion of ourselves can shade the truth about gaslighting behavior, but this book lays intentions bare.

As an author and a person who works with people of great ambition and drive, I have found that every one of us has the capacity to gaslight, but to varying degrees. The difference between all of us is that some people will welcome this manipulative and controlling streak, as long as it benefits them, while the rest of us will pull ourselves back from being manipulative in consideration of the other person. The unfortunate truth is that gaslighting has become a way of life and its effects can be felt throughout society, from politics and work relationships to, of course, personal relationships, as well. It is a learned behavior that can be acquired from childhood, especially if you were gaslit or saw it happening to a member of the household, like a parent or sibling.

Manipulation can change the way we parent, work, play, and socialize. It can and will affect our relationships with members of the opposite sex and take away the power that enables us to make informed and beneficial decisions about our lives. Imagine, for a minute, a mother experiencing gaslighting. She will not only question her reality but her decisions because of the gaslighting and this will affect her children and spouse directly, creating an unhealthy home environment. Now replace that mother with yourself and you will see that gaslighting has an effect on everyone around the affected individual because it is such an insidious form of abuse. It can take place gradually over a prolonged period of time without anyone noticing it, causing irreparable damage in some cases.

Your life can be drastically changed by the things you don't know and gaslighting in your life may be apparent or it may be hidden under the guise of love and looking out for your interests. You may not be a victim of gaslighting in your relationships, but perhaps you know someone who is. Or perhaps you have heard of someone who is. Or maybe you have interacted with a gaslighter. With gaslighting, there is often the feeling that something is wrong or the feeling you are being pushed to accept something that is not in line with your perception. Oftentimes, gaslighters are people we trust, so you don't believe they could be manipulating you. But, if you understand what gaslighting is, how it is done, and what it is meant to accomplish, you have a better chance of questioning the manipulation before it gets too far. It is safe to say that shutting down any form of gaslighting in your life or the lives of those around you can save a life.

Learning about gaslighting is an excellent place to start to help you nip such relationships in the bud before they become toxic and destructive. All the aspects of gaslighting that you need to know about are in this book and you can use it as your guide to maneuver this minefield of emotional abuse that has become an insidious part of our culture and society. But what do you do when you identify gaslighting in yourself or in others around you? Working on change is the hardest part that a gaslighter has to embrace. If this is you, let this book help you to become a leader, friend, companion, or partner who looks beyond your own intention to the good of all others around you. This book will help you understand the real impact of having power over people. You ought to get this book if you have no more intentions of being led on.

This quote by Albert Camus says it best with regards to gaslighting, "Nothing is more despicable than respect based on fear." And may I add to this, manipulation.

Enjoying this book so far? Remember to head to the bottom of this book for a bonus bite-sized yet valuable free resource on Conversational Hypnosis. This mini e-book is the easiest way to learn how to be a successful conversational hypnotist. Curious about the benefits it can do to your normal day to day conversations? Get your copy now! This free resource is available for a limited time only.

CHAPTER ONE:

Gaslighting 101

What is gaslighting?

Gaslighting is a nefarious type of psychological manipulation of an individual that makes them doubt their sanity, truth, beliefs, judgment, perception, values, and even memories. The main aim of gaslighting is to cause the person to have low esteem and/or to gain power over the person. Gaslighting happens gradually in a relationship and the actions may seem harmless in the beginning.

Gaslighters use certain very specific terms to cause confusion and muddy the waters, so the victim's perception of events seems unreliable or even fictional. They may say something like, "I don't know what you are talking about" or, "That didn't happen like that, you are just making stuff up" or, "You are just being emotional." Used frequently enough over a long period of time, the victim starts to doubt their memory, get confused about even the most obvious happenings in their lives, and more and more rely on the abuser to corroborate their reality.

Gaslighting has been a weapon used by many abusers who prefer to use emotional abuse on their victims so their actions are not easily noticeable by others. This allows them to maintain power over their victims for a longer period of time. The typical result of gaslighting is living with cognitive dissonance, which means the victim holds two different points of view at the same time that are in contradiction with each other. For example, they may recognize that the abuser is not being honest or is intentionally misleading them. But they have so much love for them that they are willing to tell themselves they must be wrong about the other person. As a result, they continue to enable the other person's abuse, which eventually whittles away their cognitive abilities.

History of gaslighting

The terminology "gaslighting" came from the 1938 play, Gaslight, also known as Angel Street, in the United States. The play, which was later adapted into movies in 1940 and 1944, was about a woman, Bella Manningham, whose husband, Jack Manningham, manipulated her into thinking she was mad. The husband literally dimmed and brightened the lights in their home and pretended that nothing happened in a bid to make the wife doubt her sanity. This play is a perfect depiction of a desolate relationship in which one party tries to undermine the other's sense of reality and, in the process, causes them mental harm. If this play is anything to go by, gaslighting has been a technique used by abusers for a long time.

Looking past this play as just another pastiche melodrama, its re-enactment by various playwrights over the years has shown that the subject matter is still relevant in modern times, especially as the techniques and tactics used in gaslighting have become more advanced. In the play, Jack Manningham also isolates his wife from her support system in order to make himself the sole interpreter of her reality. Unfortunately, in the play, his ploy works and she becomes dependent on him to discern and translate the situations in her life while, at the same time, falling more into hopelessness and despair.

Examples of gaslighting today

The gaslighting effect has appeared in decades of studies about psychoanalysis and it has also manifested itself in different TV shows over the years. One of the personalities that is considered the most prolific gaslighter of modern times is, unfortunately, the president of the United States, Donald Trump. The term gaslighting can be attached to anything that is made to sound surreal enough to cause you to question your perception of reality. There have been quite a number of gaslighting instances associated with the President of the United States, where he has tried to make his opponents seem unhinged for questioning his actions and those of his close consorts. Here are a few examples:

Brett Kavanaugh and Dr. Christine Blasey Ford

During the confirmation hearing of Brett Kavanaugh, President Donald Trump called Dr. Christine Blasey Ford's accusations that Kavanaugh had sexually assaulted her in high school fabricated and a hoax. The following remarks by the president created an atmosphere where the victim's reality was questioned and her memory challenged, just because time had passed after the fact.

The president remarked: "The American public has seen this charade, has seen this dishonesty by the Democrats. And when you mention impeach [sic] a justice of the United States Supreme Court who is a top scholar, top student, top intellect, and who did nothing wrong and there is no corroboration of any kind. It was all made up, it was fabricated. And it is a disgrace. And I think it's really going to show you something come November 6."

Somehow Brett Kavanaugh's perceived intelligence was enough to falsify everything that Dr. Ford said and it called into question the validity of her version of the events.

Donald Trump and Hilary Clinton

As a woman in a presidential race, Hilary Clinton faced quite a number of questions and a lot of scrutiny about her stand on women's issues. But when the presidential candidate tackled issues about women or stood up for women's rights, then-candidate Donald Trump accused her of playing the "woman card".

On the campaign trail, Trump kept insinuating that Clinton had no chance of winning if she wasn't playing the woman card. This argument was meant to not only invalidate the issues that Clinton focused on when it came to women, but it was also supposed to make her look like a weaker candidate who had nothing to offer the American people except her gender. This is despite the fact that Clinton served in the previous administration and was even voted as the most popular public servant of her ilk in front of President Obama and vice president Joe Biden.

In one of his rallies in Spokane Washington, Trump claimed that Clinton accused him of raising his voice while speaking to women. "She's going - did you hear that Donald Trump is raising his voice while speaking to women. Oh, I'm sorry, I'm sorry. I mean all men - we're terrified to speak to women any more - we may raise our voices."

This statement portrays Clinton as an opponent who is looking to curtail the freedoms of men and policemen in how they conduct themselves around women. It is meant to put the fear in men that women are going to gang up against them with the help of Hilary Clinton. Gaslighting Clinton worked very well with some voters, who bought into his portrayal of her as the beginning of the end of the natural order of things as they knew it. It played to their gender resentment and gender bias, especially in homes where the woman made more money than the man.

Donald Trump's incivility when he talked about Clinton and his constant accusing her of playing the woman card was meant to diminish her worth as a leader to the voters and, unfortunately, many voters bought into this argument. In this case, Donald Trump succeeded in gaslighting the American people and Hilary Clinton. He effectively changed the perception of reality for voters, making them feel like he was the only solution to keep things in their "natural order". He also managed to gaslight Clinton by making her look like an unworthy candidate because she cared about matters like childcare and pay equality for women. This tactic was actually meant to keep Clinton silent about women's issues because Trump didn't feel like he had a handle on them and he couldn't try and become an advocate for women so late in the game after his Access Hollywood tape.

As a gaslighter, in this case, Donald Trump was trying to silence Clinton's arguments by painting her standards and opinions as oppressive and unreasonable.

Kellie Sutton and Steven Gane

Kellie Sutton was not a famous person, but a 30-year-old mother of three who lived with a bully of a boyfriend, Steven Gane. But in a landmark case that punished the gaslighters, Steven Gane received a sentence of four years and three months. He was also slapped with a criminal behavior order that will last for 10 years from 2018. This order requires Gane to notify the police of any sexual relationship that he has that lasts more than 14 days. The notification must be done within 21 days of the beginning of any relationship.

In this case, Steven Gane was found guilty of using coercive and controlling behavior within an intimate relationship, assaulting the victim by beating and assault occasioning actual bodily harm. According to the judge in the case, Phillip Grey, the abuser wormed his way into her affections and home and then sought to control and dominate her. The judge said that Gane treated her like a meal ticket that was his to control, treated her as a possession, beat her, ground her down and broke her spirit. He further said, "Her (Kellie) texts and Facebook messages show the contempt and hostility with which you treated her. You regard women as objects you wish to use. You even referred to Miss Sutton in abusive and crude terms after her death. Your behavior drove Miss Sutton to take her own life. She threatened to kill herself and you told her to do everyone a favor and go ahead and do it."

Gane admitted he was a jealous man and his gaslighting actions were meant to exert control over his lover. According to Kellie Sutton's mother, Pamela Taylor, she was a bubbly, happy person who was funny, affectionate, and caring. However, she changed after getting into a relationship with Gane and became withdrawn and anxious.

This is the first time a conviction has been made for a gaslighting offense following the death of a victim. In the United Kingdom, the coercive and controlling legislation came into effect in 2015 and police have hailed this move as a milestone. This legislation is a section of the Serious Crime Act of 2015.

Gane and Sutton were together for only five months. In typical gaslighter behavior, he ingratiated himself to his victim by moving into her house and doing the things she needed to be done around the house, as well as buying stuff for her. This was a ploy to get her to become reliant on him. As time went by, he pulled her away from her family and friends, became more controlling even beating her when she went out without telling him where she was going. The victim hid the reality from her family and even when she eventually took her own life, they were unaware of the gaslighting going on in her life.

Steven Gane exhibited typical gaslighting behavior in controlling and coercing his partner. But in his case, it was a lethal combination of emotional and physical abuse. According to her friends, he saw the vulnerability in the single mother of three and capitalized on it. Gaslighters will always look for a weakness and exploit it to their advantage.

Russia gaslighting Americans

Since the 2016 election, Americans have been gaslit by the Russian propaganda machine that seeks to dismiss the perception that Russia manipulated the American electorate and changed the course of American politics, as if it was a figment of their imagination. Russian agents hacked into the Clinton campaign, as well as the Democratic National Committee and Democratic Congressional Campaign Committee with the aim of releasing sensitive information from the campaign. They also spread propaganda about Clinton on Twitter, Facebook, and Instagram and even staged campaign rallies in

Pennsylvania and Florida. All of this information is corroborated by the United States Intelligence Community.

However, when asked about their interference in the American elections, Russian President Vladimir Putin denied everything and instead pointed a confusing finger at their neighbor, Ukraine. In the typical deflecting behavior of a gaslighter, Russia's president pretended not to know or understand that his agents, using cyber tactics, introduced false narratives into the 2016 U.S. election which favored Donald Trump and caused damage to the Clinton campaign.

The main reason for this manipulation was to ensure the election of a candidate they could manipulate into the highest office and wield power over him. Clinton was tough on Russia and supported the sanctions in place against the country for their actions in Ukraine. When found out, Russia pointed a finger elsewhere and also began a campaign of discrediting the U.S. Intelligence Community, using their own president, no less.

U.S. Special Counsel Robert Muller uncovered evidence of a Kremlin-led operation to interfere with the elections. He also found out that 12 Russian intelligence officers infiltrated democratic emails and used phony social media accounts in order to spread divisive narratives. By 2017, 56 percent of American's believed that Russia interfered in the election, but this also means that 44 percent didn't. This is a huge percentage and it represents a large number of people who have had their perception of reality interfered with by statements like these from Putin and Donald Trump.

Putin said, "We don't have and never had any plans to interfere in U.S. domestic politics." But, according to Putin, their government can't stop private citizens from expressing their views online about U.S. politics and its developments. "How can we ban them from doing that? Do you have such a ban with regard to Russia?"

Trump: "I don't believe they interfered." In another instance, he said "Knowing something about hacking, if you don't catch the hacker in the act, it's a very hard thing to say who did the hacking. With that being said, I have to go with Russia. Could've been China, could've been a lot of different groups."

By casting aspersions on the validity of the claims, as both presidents did, and as people in high authority holding a lot of sway, the two leaders gaslit the American people into thinking that their perception of reality was not accurate. Notice that not only did they deny the action, they also pointed at other potential perpetrators. This helped them advance an alternative narrative for those who believed the hacking took place. They both understood that the facts pointed to hacking. However, deflecting the blame from Russia is just as important as denying the claim. This tactic of muddying the waters works very well for gaslighters because their victims can often barely find the grounds to make accusations stick.

Charles Manson and the Manson family

Charles Manson was a prolific gaslighter that took gaslighting tactics to the next level by influencing well-educated people to leave their lives behind. He then unleashed them onto the world to commit murder for him. Like most gaslighters, Manson portrayed himself as the next savior of the world and the rest of the world as misfits and sycophants. Most people thought that Manson was going around recruiting teenage serial killers. In fact, he was meeting the needs of vulnerable young women and, depending on their vulnerability, he exploited their specific need.

For example, if a young woman was looking for spiritual guidance, he would offer that in his warped form. If she needed a father figure, he would act in such a manner that she would find fatherly comfort from him. Not only did this make them exceedingly reliant on him, but by making them a part of each other's lives, he gave them a family and a connection that most were missing. He even called his cult the "Manson family".

Manson made them a part of his life and, for the first year in 1968, there was a deep sense of family, affection, and fulfillment between them all. Unfortunately, the years spent with Manson were in a haze of drugs, so different people in the cult remember the events differently. The timeline of the Manson story spanned two years and, by mid-1969, Manson had started ordering members of his family to kill people for him. The first victim was a friend of the Manson family by the name of Gary Hinman, who was killed by members of the family because he failed to give Manson money. The next person on his hit list was Roman Polanski, a famous film director, and his wife was the unfortunate victim. Polanski's home was targeted because a music producer who had rejected Manson lived there previously.

Having manipulated the members of his family into regarding him as their messiah, he advanced what is known as his Helter-Skelter Theory. This theory advanced the notion that African-Americans and whites would have a race war that would see thousands perish. Manson planned for the family to disappear into caves to emerge when the war was over, in order to rule the world. But when his music career flopped, he told his members that they would have to start helter-skelter themselves by committing crimes in upscale neighborhoods. This was to demonstrate to the African American community how to carry out the violence. However, clearly the murders were revenge killings for Manson against people who didn't help advance his music career.

The men and women used by Manson all completely relied on him for their understanding of reality as translated by him. In their eyes, he was not an abuser. Instead, they saw a charismatic and inspiring leader with the vision and purpose to transform their lives and humanity for the better. This trait is known as optimism bias, in which victims look on the bright side of things, even when there are clear discrepancies in the behavior of the abuser. Optimism bias exists in all of us, but it becomes more pronounced in victims of gaslighting.

Love Island's Adam and Rosie

In 2018, participants in the show Love Island, Adam and Rosie, showed how gaslighting can become a part of dating life. Viewers were concerned about how Adam used very typical gaslighting tactics on his then partner, Rosie, making her feel like she was the reason for his pursuing the new girl on the show. Adam told Rosie that he was dumping her because she was acting like a child. The failure to take responsibility for his actions and, instead, putting it on Rosie, made her feel like she was responsible for his bad behavior.

By trivializing the reaction of his partner based on his actions, Adam showed gaslighting behavior. And, apparently, when he was in a relationship with another participant by the name of Kendall, he also used gaslighting tactics on her. For example, he would say to her, "I've done nothing to make you think that I would pick someone else." This, despite the fact that he was carrying on with Rosie at the time. And the fact that he exhibited gaslighting behavior with Kendall and with Rosie every time he was interested in someone new, showed a pattern in his behavior.

Gaslighting has been seen on the show with other participants, like Joe Garratt. Garratt famously made his partner Lucie Donlan feel there was something wrong with her for being friendly with the male participants on the show, in particular Joe's rival. In his words to her, "I'm not happy with it. It's strange. I think it is time for you to get close to the girls." Joe received a lot of backlash for his gaslighting of Lucie and was voted off the show. But more importantly, he had to be whisked off to a safe house as a result.

When intimate feelings are involved, gaslighting can be a gateway to an abusive relationship and it can quickly morph into physical abuse. The victim is likely to stay in an unhealthy relationship because they have become comfortable with the nature of the relationship. With time, the abusive pattern continues and escalates.

CHAPTER TWO:

The Gaslighter's Tale

Narcissism is at the core of gaslighting behavior. In each of the examples I gave in the previous chapter, the gaslighters feel superior to the victim and believe the victim should look up to only them. Because they can't achieve this naturally, they resort to coercive and manipulative behavior to erode the confidence of the victim and make them question their perception and judgment calls. This effectively puts the victim in a vulnerable position, which the gaslighter can then exploit by making themselves seem like the be-all, end-all to the victim.

Inside the mind of a gaslighter

When dealing with a gaslighter, you will find out there are those who understand what they are doing and those who aren't even aware of their actions. Famous gaslighters, like Charles Manson, did not just embark on a journey to recruit and manipulate young women out of the blue. Manson took a class that was based on Dale Carnegie's book "How to Win Friends and Influence People". The manipulation tactics he used on his followers were learned from this book. This book wasn't written with nefarious manipulation in mind. In fact, some of the world's greatest minds, like Warren Buffet, have also benefited from the teachings in this book. But Manson applied the techniques in an evil manner to suit his own needs.

This is a classic example of a gaslighter who intentionally learned how to manipulate people, applied the tactics they learned, and used them for their own means. Some gaslighters are aware of their behavior and willfully target vulnerable people whom they can easily control.

The opposite of this is a gaslighter who is not truly aware of their actions. This is especially true of authoritarian personalities who tend to think in absolutes. To them, things are black or white, so the other person either does what they say or does not. These are the hardest types of gaslighters to help because they do not identify themselves as having a problem. The result is, however, the same for both the aware and unaware gaslighter - they get a payoff when their victim becomes completely reliant on them. They both want to have control over their victim's thoughts, whether they feel like they are doing it for their good or for their own benefit.

The gaslighter personality

The gaslighter personality is typically found in people who have two contradictory issues at play within themselves. They have self-esteem and self-worth issues and the only way for them to feel in control is by manipulating people and the situations around them to favor them. But they also have an inflated sense of importance. This makes them feel in charge of their own lives and also very entitled. The gaslighter can be either a schemer and a master at distorting the facts, or they can be an overbearing authority figure who doesn't like to be questioned and sees things only through their personal prism.

Narcissism plays a huge role in gaslighting behavior because it helps the gaslighter to mask their insecurity. Narcissism is a personality disorder in which a person has an inflated sense of their own worth and importance. They also have an insatiable and deeply entrenched need for admiration and attention, plus a complete lack of empathy for others. At the slightest criticism, a narcissistic person will lose their mask of self-confidence, sometimes resulting in violence because their insecure side is suddenly exposed. For such people, any actions by the victim, like questioning a decision or even asking for clarification, can be considered a criticism, making them lash out at the victim.

For example, if a wife asks a gaslighter husband about his spending of the family income, the man may feel like she is questioning his ability to make good decisions. As a narcissist, he will take this as an insult and may become abusive in that instant. It is very easy for a person with a narcissist personality disorder to become a gaslighter because of their sense of entitlement and preoccupation with being admired. On the flip side, a person with a gaslighter personality also exhibits behaviors like being withdrawn and moody when things don't go their way. In addition, they experience difficulty adapting to any changes in their environment. They also secretly have feelings of shame and insecurity over certain aspects of their lives. Some gaslighters can also suffer from depression, which makes them more likely to abuse alcohol and drugs.

Ultimately, the gaslighter personality has a persistent urge as part of their behavior to control others around them by any means necessary.

Why they do it

The main reason why gaslighters go to the lengths they do to control people is because of the power it gives them. The need for dominance helps them feel good about themselves because they are already dealing with feelings of insecurity and low self-esteem in themselves. The gaslighter may try to frame their actions as being of benefit to the victim, but they are, in fact, for their own benefit.

There are cases when people will gaslight someone close to them in order to cover up a misdeed, like an affair or drug use. In such a situation, the gaslighter is not your typical narcissist. Instead, because they are afraid of the repercussions of their behavior, they will make the other person question their reality to protect themselves. The one thing to recognize is that no matter the reason why one is gaslighting, their sole intention is to benefit themselves at the expense of the other person.

Gaslighters also like to use these techniques to feel a sense of security, especially if they have grown up with some level of insecurity in their environment. Because gaslighting is a learned behavior, the abuser uses it as reflex protective behavior to protect their feelings and help them feel in control of their life. This learned behavior is picked up from their environment and, when they see that it works, they will try it on their first victim. If they successfully manipulate people around them, it becomes a cognitive strategy for survival.

Gaslighter confessions

It is crucial to understand that gaslighters are human beings too, despite their behavior. They crave self-preservation and acceptance, which they honestly believe their actions bring to them. It is because of this need for acceptance and belonging that gaslighters may continue to gaslight their loved ones, despite seeing their suffering. They may be afraid of being alone or looking like a loser. As a result, their self-preservation takes precedence over any feelings of guilt or empathy.

As an author who has listened to many stories about gaslighting from both victims and abusers, I have heard gut-wrenching stories that leave fully functional men and women with debilitating fears and anxieties for a long time and, in some cases, even for the rest of their lives. One such story that I came across was in BBC Stories and it involves a Canadian lawyer by the name of Greg and several women he gaslit in during their relationships.

During therapy, Greg realized that he was a gaslighter and, on further probing, connected the beginning of his behavior to a relationship he had at the age of 21. Greg is a self-confessed serial gaslighter with 11 relationships under his belt and he used gaslighting techniques on each of the women. By the age of 28, he recognized the gaslighting pattern in his relationships and he spoke out in order to help women identify the telltale signs of a gaslighter.

His first relationship as a law undergrad was with a master's degree student by the name of Paula. He was unfaithful, carrying on several affairs behind her back, but she was intelligent enough to know what he was up to. Greg didn't want to break up with her, but neither did he want to give up his other lovers, so he resorted to gaslighting her to create uncertainty in her mind about what he was up to.

One of the ways he created an alternative reality is by making her question her relationship with social media. He started to pretend she had an obsession with social media. To make his statements more palatable to Paula's intelligence, he started off by making it a joke about how crazy she was about social media. Greg was leaving a footprint of his infidelity on social media. With time, he started using demeaning language when she raised issues about his social media use, making her feel like she was just being dramatic and paranoid about what she saw. He would act like it was a joke, whenever she confronted him.

The constant gaslighting made Paula start to doubt what she was seeing, believing she was overreacting and not confronting compromising situations for the fear of being too dramatic. So she apologized for doubting him and promised to spend less time on social media. This gave Greg the freedom to continue with his lifestyle. He was at the beginning of the gaslighting behavior pattern, in which one uses lies and exaggeration to offer an alternative narrative. The more extreme end of the spectrum involves using controlling, coercive, manipulative, and sometimes even physical means to dominate the other person.

According to Greg, despite Paula being a feminist and well-educated, she believed the narrative he fed her about the other women being the liars and people who couldn't be trusted. As a result, she resented the other women and even when she met them and found out they were good people, Greg's version still won the day. With this gaslighting tactic, Greg was effectively isolating her from others who could tell her the truth, all while feeding her anxiety about what she saw on social media.

Greg chose the type of woman that most people would assume would not be affected by emotional abuse. He said he targeted highly successful and intelligent women who are actually even more receptive to being gaslit compared to their less successful counterparts. Such women tend to be conscientious and generally do the right thing, making them trustworthy and willing to trust others more easily. They are also agreeable and empathetic to a fault. These are typically the qualities that have made them successful in their careers, but they can be exploited, making them vulnerable to gaslighting.

According to Greg, many abusers approach relationships with a checklist or a blueprint of what they can target to make that person more vulnerable. He said that his victims all came with an idea of what they thought a successful relationship should look like, often depictions from movies and fairytale love stories. He further explains that, as a gaslighter, you look at this narrative the victim wants the relationship to follow and you set about laying it out, but to fit your own needs. You then begin to do things over a period of time that supports the narrative you want the victim to fall for.

Greg claims that, although he wasn't physically abusive or aggressive with any of the women, looking back he understands the damage he did was psychological. His advice to women who are seeing signs of gaslighting in their relationship is to talk to male friends. He explains that male friends are likely to notice gaslighting behavior in other men and are likely to be brutally honest with their female friends. Female friends, on the other hand, can be intimidated easily and are likely to tell the victim what she wants to hear. In fact, he was wary of his ex-girlfriend's male friends because he knew they could see right through his tactics.

As a man, talking about getting gaslit is almost taboo, as most people feel a man can't be abused by his partner, especially if it's a woman. Many men suffer gaslighting at the hands of their wives and girlfriends for years before they can even bring themselves to accept what is going on. This shows that gaslighting is not confined to women as the victims, alone.

In the same BBC series, I came across the story of an American man whose wife gaslit him, traumatizing him for many years. If he made plans with his friends, she would bring up an argument, preventing him from going out and later feign not recalling he was supposed to meet his friends. She would call his work and act like something was wrong at home and, when he came home, she would accuse him of overreacting, acting like she didn't make it sound serious. In the end, he lost his job because of these incidences.

She would hang up a picture and when he complimented it, she would claim it had been hanging up for over two weeks and she couldn't believe his stupidity at not noticing it. He began to doubt his memories because of such things since he couldn't remember seeing it before.

Unfortunately, help for men in abusive relationships is far less, compared to resources for women. Men are expected to put their foot down to stop the abuse. But the truth is that gaslighting happens to all genders and the effects are equally devastating.

Are you a gaslighter?

If you have doubts about whether you are a gaslighter, this simple question may be the first place to start:

Do you put down your partner or child or any other person close to you, wait for their response, and then attack their response, making them feel incapable of making a sound judgment call? You may believe that their judgment was flawed concerning a particular subject. However, if you make this a constant habit, where you make the other person doubt their ability to make sound decisions, you are a gaslighter. The unaware gaslighter may think they are just being reasonable or being honest. Such people believe in being brutally honest, only they are just being brutal in their control of the other person. They may tell you that they are rational and cool-headed and don't like expressions of anxiety. You can expect them to say things like, "You are being too sensitive" because they feel justified to say whatever they want to say in their abrasive manner.

The aware gaslighter, on the other hand, is very methodical in how they set up their victims for the fall. They will begin by being extra nice or helpful and gain the other person's trust. Their jabs will at first come as jokes or a guilt trip. The gradual escalation into full-blown domination and gaslighting takes months or even years.

Another question to ask yourself is, "Do you ever use phrases that make the person question themselves? For example, do you call them crazy? Or call their friends or family crazy? By making them feel like they are irrational in their thoughts, opinions, choice of friends, or even hobbies, you are gaslighting the person.

For a gaslighter, every act of control, coercion, and domination over their victim is a power trip and this can become addictive. This is why they will use the victim's smallest actions to make them feel like they are not acting rationally.

The final question to ask yourself is, "Do you feel insecure about yourself and derive comfort from making the other person question themselves?" With this question, it is important to investigate whether you are just an emotional abuser who likes to have control over how your partner feels or a gaslighter who wants to go the extra mile and discredit them by making the person question their sanity.

Three types of gaslighters

Psychoanalysts have, over the years, identified three types of gaslighters based on their behavior patterns. Respected voices in this field, like the Associate Director of the Yale Center for Emotional Intelligence, Dr. Robin Stern, have taken over two and a half decades to learn about the effects of these gaslighters and their specific tactics on their victims. Here is what you need to know about these three types:

The Glamour Gaslighter

The Glamour Gaslighter always starts out as a gentleman, which is meant to sweep his victim off their feet. If it is a woman, they will be elegant and charming, sometimes even delicate and dainty in her actions. She may act like a damsel in distress, needing her victim's manly attributes to come to her rescue. The male Glamour Gaslighter will buy expensive gifts and take the victim to the best restaurants, making her feel like she is the center of his world

Not only does he target her but also her loved ones, from friends to family, making her the envy of everyone in her circle. But in small ways, he begins to control her. In the beginning, it may be scheduling activities together that coincide with plans she has made with family or friends. This forces her to choose him over them. He will drop subtle remarks like, "Well, I guess spending time with me is not as important to you as it is to me." Some may try to instill the fear of a break up by saying, "It's okay. Go hang out with your friends. I will take so and so...full disclosure though...we had a thing before I met you and she still holds a candle for me." This is meant to make the victim feel insecure and jealous enough to make the victim abandon her plans for his.

In the same scenario, the female Glamour Gaslighter may dress provocatively to go out after finding out that the man has made plans to hang out with his friends. She will let him know that she is going out with an ex-boyfriend or a colleague from work, making it clear that her date has feelings for her. The aim of her actions is to make him jealous enough to abandon his plans. Suddenly, she is furious at him for overreacting and causing her to feel guilty about wanting to go out to have a good time. She blames him for being manipulative and he is forced to placate her and assure her that this wasn't his intention, all the while he is wondering if he overreacted and whether he caused her to change her plans for him.

The male Glamour Gaslighter will abruptly become furious at his partner for the smallest of things, like laughing at a joke with his friend, wanting to pay for something when they are together or even giving a male friend a hug. The accusations will range from trying to show him up in public to not behaving like a good girlfriend. Of course, the woman is unsure of what she has done wrong and the more she tries to argue her case, the more she seems to upset him. To bring back the peace in the relationship, she will immediately try to make things right between them by apologizing and promising to be more considerate. After all, he is a good man and she just made him angry with her actions.

This pattern continues where the original love comes back intermittently, but most of the time the gaslighter is controlling their partner with their actions and words.

The Intimidator Gaslighter

This type of gaslighter is a bully, who uses aggression and even physical dominance to get his way. The Intimidator Gaslighter is typically male because he has the physical strength to make his victim do his bidding or resort to violence. With the Intimidator, there are no subtle references to what they want. Rather, he is abusive and will show aggression in public,

Such gaslighters are prone to sulking, silent treatment, threats, and playing on their partner's deepest fears to get their way. For example, they will threaten to take the kids away because their partner took the kids out of the house without his permission. If the partner's deepest fear is being a failure as a parent, they will use this fear by saying something like, "You act just like your mom and you know how she was. I don't think you are a good mother to my kids and I will take them away from you." The victim, out of desperation, promises to ask his permission to take the kids out. She will start to believe that her parenting skills are not up to par, which causes her anxiety.

The Intimidator Gaslighter will continually bully the victim, even in the presence of other people, often putting her down in public.

The Good Guy Gaslighter

This gaslighter is loved by the victim's family and friends tell her that she is lucky and will not find someone like him again. They act like an amazing guy or woman in public, treating their partners with respect and affection, but behind closed doors, the façade drops and they become vicious. The problem with this kind of gaslighter is that their actions in public discredit any attempts by the victim to paint a different picture. The Good Guy Gaslighter relies on public perception to keep their actions hidden. The victims are usually afraid or ashamed to tell on the gaslighter and, because of this, the abuser can get away with years of abuse without anyone knowing what is happening.

For example, a Good Guy Gaslighter may be having a meal with his girlfriend and she sees a male friend. He comes over to their table, where she stands up to give him a hug. Unlike the Intimidator Gaslighter, who may storm off at this gesture and show aggression to his partner in public, the Good Guy Gaslighter will reach out for a handshake, introduce himself, invite the friend to join them and proceed to be charming and even friendly. However, inside he or she is seething and neither the girlfriend nor the friend can tell. At the earliest opportunity, behind closed doors, he will accuse her of flirting with the man, having an affair, and making a fool of him. Why? Because of the way they hugged or how they looked at each other. He makes her promise not to see her friend again.

The victim starts to believe that maybe she lingered on the hug or maybe she was too attentive when her friend was speaking. She will apologize and promise to not have any interaction with the friend. And she may even stop hugging male friends altogether because of this.

CHAPTER THREE:

Dancing With the Devil

See the signs

Being in love can be great but the important thing is not to lose yourself in the process of loving another. The signs of gaslighting can be seen clearly if one knows what to look for. You can look for these signs in all types of relationships, from intimate, family, business, and even friendships.

Subtle signs of gaslighting you won't even notice

Like I mentioned previously, gaslighting is gradual and, in most cases, a subtle form of emotional abuse that can take place over years, leaving the victim completely disoriented because of the erosion of their sense of reality. These are some of the techniques gaslighters use:

Blatant lies

Gaslighting is based on blatant lies told by the abuser to the victim to throw them off-kilter. By introducing a huge deliberate lie, the abuser lays the groundwork for tearing down the victim's perception of reality. Usually, the victim can tell she or he is being lied to, but because the lie is being told with a straight face and the abuser is sticking to their alternative facts, the victim's sense of reality is thrown off and they begin to doubt their own version of events. One lie after another will soon erode the victim's sense of reality, keeping them reliant on the abuser for the "correct" reality.

Lying is one of the key behaviors in gaslighting. We can even say with certainty that for gaslighting to occur, the abuser must use blatant lies.

Countering

This technique involves the abuser telling the victim that they remember something incorrectly. This usually happens when both the victim and the abuser have experienced the same event or the victim has seen something the abuser has done that is not in line with their expectations of their partner. Usually whatever has transpired is not a pleasant event.

The abuser will typically try to undermine the credibility of the victim's memory of the event. To do this, they will counter their version of events by providing an alternative narrative. With this technique, there is a semblance of subtlety, meaning the general description of the experience will be similar to a large extent, but the areas that portray the abuser in a bad light will be omitted or tweaked to be favorable. For example, a woman sees her husband having dinner with another woman after he told her he would be at a business meeting that evening. Upon confronting him, he concurs he was having dinner with a woman, but she was the client he was meeting and what seemed like an intimate conversation was just him being attentive because the business deal is crucial for the company.

Trivializing

Gaslighters like to trivialize the issues that matter to the victim. This is effective in making the victim feel like their opinion or perception is inconsequential. It works extremely well, leaving the victim with low self-esteem and self-worth. Isolating someone who feels unworthy is easier because they already believe that they don't matter and no one will miss them.

When they are not trivializing matters, they are usually pretending not to understand why the issue matters to the victim. For example, if one person is gaslighting another about finances, every time the other person asks about their finances, the abuser will say something along the lines of "I don't know why you are worried about my spending when I have told you we are financially stable." Or, "Why are you questioning me about money when you know how bad you are with finances."

Discrediting

Discrediting the victim is a ploy right out of the gaslighter's playbook. This tactic entails convincing the people around you that you are unstable and insane. Good Guy Gaslighters and Glamour Gaslighters are quite good at convincing the victim's loved ones that they are a good fit for their partner. This is one of the reasons why gaslighting victims may not want to talk to their loved ones about what goes on behind closed doors.

Sometimes, even parents and siblings are so blinded by the charm of the abuser that they fail to notice the pain and suffering of their own loved ones. In some cases, the victim's support system is so completely overtaken by the abuser that people in the support system begin to gaslight the victim, as well.

Stonewalling

This involves the abuser completely shutting out the victim by not engaging them in conversation or refusing to listen to them entirely. They may also change the subject so they don't have to address the issue their partner is trying to raise. Usually, this tactic lays the ground for the abuser to play the victim and place the fault for the disagreement on the victim.

For example, if a man asks his gaslighting wife where she was and why she didn't come back home last night, the wife can refuse to answer or refuse to listen to him and walk out of the room. When she comes back into the room, she will talk to him about dinner plans she is arranging for him and their friends. Now, if the man tries to steer the conversation back to the issue of her staying out all night, she will make him feel guilty for not appreciating the effort she is putting in order to create a fun time with him and their friends. She will probably say something like, "I can't believe how selfish you are, not even appreciating my efforts towards this dinner. Instead, you want to make me feel guilty about going out to have a little fun with my friends. I am sure I told you about last night a couple of days ago, but now you pretend that you can't remember."

The man will feel conflicted because she is clearly doing something nice for him with regard to the dinner. And he will also question himself about forgetting or not concentrating when she mentioned the dinner when she said she did.

Reframing

Gaslighters are very good at twisting the thoughts and experiences of the victim in favor of their narrative. This contributes to the victim questioning their reality and relying on the perspective of the abuser. Let's go back to the example of the woman who saw her partner at dinner with another woman. When confronted, the man can try to reframe the experience and twist the thoughts of the woman by saying something like, "We were both there and indeed I was having dinner with her. But surely, you are not suggesting that we shouldn't interact with other women or men just because we are seeing each other? I wouldn't do that to you."

Of course, the woman will quickly try to clarify that she is not against him having female interactions and then she questions whether she was reading too much into what she saw. He has succeeded in twisting her thoughts and making it seem like she is implying that she doesn't want him to have any interactions with other females. Because she says he is free to talk to other women, he will take advantage of this while always reminding her that she said she was okay with him having female friends.

Fake compassion

This is a very popular tactic, especially in the early days of gaslighting in a relationship. Since the victim is not yet under the abuser's thumb, he or she will try to claim everything they do is for the well-being of the victim. This tactic ingratiates the abuser to the victim and helps them gain the victim's trust. With time, they will begin to tell the victim what to do under the guise of being protective or having their best interests at heart.

In the beginning, the abuser will start by saying, "I don't want to tell you what to do, but I strongly care about you and I just want to make sure you are okay. If you ask me, you would be better off not being friends with X." As the relationship progresses and the victim can be controlled this phrase will change into, "I have always told you to put a stop to that friendship because I am just looking out for you. But you think I am trying to control you. Now look, she is coming between us." Fake compassion is a deadly tactic that is used to isolate the victim from friends and family.

Easy to spot warning signs that you are being manipulated by a gaslighter

You have proof of something yet they still deny it:

Gaslighters are focused on altering your reality, so even if you have proof of what they said, they will deny it and even accuse you of trying to alter their reality. They can be very believable in their denial and will pretend that they don't know what you are talking about to the extent that you begin to wonder if you are wrong.

They use your fears, failures, and doubts as ammunition:

When your partner uses negative and sometimes even positive aspects of your life to manipulate you, this is a gaslighting relationship. For example, they know how important a promotion, your family, your children, or your career is to you and they use this to manipulate you. They will tell you how unworthy you are because you failed to get that promotion or your career isn't progressing and so forth.

In most cases, gaslighters use the most intimate things you share with them to make you feel unworthy. These are among the first things they will attack, in order to control you and your response to them.

They constantly lie

They will lie about everything, usually either a lie here and there to support their narrative or undermine your credibility with yourself and others. These lies wear down the victim and, before long, it seems as though only the abuser sees things clearly in the relationship.

They occasionally use positive reinforcement

"See, that's not bad at all. You did that very well because you listened to what I said. Good job, honey." Using positive reinforcement throws the victim off-kilter and they see the man, woman, parent, or partner they once knew. This makes them feel that the abuser is not so bad. As long as the victim does what they are told, everything will be just fine. Looking closely at the action that prompted the positive reinforcement, you will notice that it serves the abuser.

They project their flaws onto their victim

The gaslighter is often dealing with unsavory issues, like infidelity, substance abuse, and violence, among other things. So, as a distraction from their own behavior, they will project it onto their victim. For example, if he or she is cheating, they will accuse the victim of cheating in order to draw attention away from their own infidelity.

They tell others that their victim is not stable

Maligning you to others is a tactic that a gaslighter will use so they can gain support for their actions. If they tell your mutual friend you have a bad temper, the next time you react to something they say in public in the presence of that mutual friend, it will reinforce the gaslighter's words and you look like the one with a problem. Soon enough, the gaslighter will tell you that even the mutual friend concurs you have a problem. That doesn't mean that the other person said that (remember gaslighters are blatant liars), but you are led to believe that others see you as problematic, as well.

Gaslighters know that confusion is the best way to disorient their victim and keep him or her in their clutches. Therefore, they are very strategic about sowing confusion in their relationship, while having the upper hand with the correct information. To achieve a good level of confusion, they will paint everyone related to the victim as a liar, so the victim is always relying on them for the truth.

It is crucial to be aware of gaslighting techniques, so you can start to identify them if they happen to occur in your relationship.

Questions to ask yourself to assess if you have a gaslighter in your life

As mentioned above, a gaslighting relationship is peppered with constant confusion and emotional turmoil. This is because what you see and what you hear from your loved one feeds two very different realities. You need an effective and efficient way to be able to tell whether you are in a relationship with a gaslighter. Introspection is important, but don't forget to also look at the other person's behavior. Here are some questions to get you started:

- Do you often wonder whether you are too sensitive because of the things your partner says? But yet you don't have this problem with other people?

- Is your personal definition of yourself something you identified or was it pointed out by your partner?
- Do you feel confused even about the most basic information or timeline of events?
- Do you have the tendency to second guess yourself since you entered into the relationship? To the extent of stifling your opinions because you are unsure of yourself?
- Are you always apologizing to the other person, even when you have not done anything that warrants an apology?
- Do you consider yourself lucky to have the other person, but you are still unhappy and you can't figure out why?
- Are you the excuse-maker in chief for the other person's actions?
- Do you live a double life because of their actions to avoid criticism? For example, do you act like you are living your dream life with the Glamour Gaslighter just to keep up appearances with friends, co-workers, and family members?
- Do you question your worth in your relationship or at work?
- Do you feel like you can't get anything right?
- Do you feel like there is something wrong with your relationship, but you can't point out what it is?
- Are you lying to your partner to avoid sarcastic responses, put-downs, and to maintain the peace in the relationship?

You will notice that all these questions tend to revolve around your reality, instincts, sanity, and feelings. They show you whether you have lost yourself to your partner. Also, note that these questions are very specific to your mental well-being.

Why do victims still choose to stay?

Gaslighting is a very painful reality to accept. Accepting that the person you trust and love and shared intimate moments with is trying to make you lose your mental stability isn't something that anyone wants to hear. In most cases, gaslighters have seen the signs mentioned above or they have been warned by friends and family or even the abuser's previous partner.

The victim needs to understand that it is not their fault and the gaslighting is a reflection of the abuser. In the words of Wayne Dyer, self-help book author, "How people treat you is their karma. How you react is yours." Victims of gaslighting may choose to stay in the relationship for a couple of reasons, including:

Societal expectations

Even though we live in a society where men and women are redefining how they want to live by living single lives or having open relationships, the majority of the population still holds on to the traditional sense of a relationship. This means that it still matters to many people to be in a monogamous relationship, sharing assets, children, and companionship for the rest of their lives.

These societal expectations make it hard for many victims to walk away from gaslighting relationships because they are afraid to lose their standing in society. They are also afraid to lose the feeling of being loved and attached to someone they care about, despite the fact that there is no love there. The fear of the stigma of divorce in some cultures is greater than the fear of living with an abusive partner.

It also doesn't help matters when society promotes a ride-or-die mentality. Even in love songs or romantic flicks, the woman, especially, will call herself the "ride-or-die chick." This mentality is typically not expected of men in society. This is a woman who will stand by their man through all manner of shenanigans.

Normalization of abuse

If the victim has lived in an abusive relationship for a long time, they may begin to normalize the behavior. Since gaslighting is an insidious and gradual form of abuse, the victim can slowly and unknowingly normalize the behavior or their partner by rationalizing it. Take, for example, an abuser who uses the fake compassion technique, in which they tell their victim they are only looking out for them or doing something for their good. The victim will come to associate the harmful behavior, like isolation or even physical violence, with love and care. This makes it hard for them to seek help because they no longer see anything wrong with what their partner is doing.

Physical danger

Gaslighters are capable of going to any lengths to keep their victim or keep their behavior a secret. The loss of power over their victim reinforces the gaslighter's feelings of insecurity and low self-esteem. They are likely to want to preserve their status in the abusive environment and also in society. As a result, they can become physically violent with the victim and may even go as far as killing them.

In some cases, the gaslighter will threaten to harm themselves if the victim leaves, putting the burden of their well-being on the victim. Who wants to be responsible for another human being's death, especially when you are already vulnerable and depleted yourself? Statistics from domestic environment organizations show that women are up to 70 times more likely to be killed within the next few weeks after leaving an abusive relationship. So, when a woman leaves a relationship, she has to create a safety plan to get out of reach of the abuser.

Eroded self-worth

The actions of the gaslighter over time will erode the self-esteem and self-worth of the victim. He or she is left feeling like they aren't good enough at anything or for anything. By eroding the victim's self-worth, the abuser makes the victim dependent on them to define who they are. And, since in many gaslighting relationships, the abuser makes the victim feel like there is no one who will love them because they are damaged goods, the person being gaslit will continue to stay.

Plus, it is hard to escape the pattern of control that has taken place over the years and has become a part of the victim's life. This is one of the reasons why a victim will probably go back to the abuser when he or she pleads for them to come back. Statistics show that a person in an abusive relationship will try to leave up to seven times before finally leaving for good.

The make-up honeymoon phase

Every so often in a gaslighting relationship, the victim catches a glimpse of the person they fell in love with and this is usually during an apology after an abusive situation. This is the typical cycle of abuse and it is aimed at getting their victim to let down their guard and minimize the abusive incident. The honeymoon stage is short-lived, however, as the abuser needs to maintain control of the victim and, to do this, they have to keep them feeling downtrodden.

During the make-up honeymoon period, the abuser is particularly attentive to the needs of the victim. They will buy them gifts, help with chores, and show love and affection. But they will still stay true to their gaslighting behavior by making the victim acknowledge how lucky they are to have them in their life and how things would be like that every day if only she or he behaved.

Remember the pattern of behavior of a gaslighter includes ingratiating themselves to their victim so they are blinded by the actions of love.

Hope for better

The victim always lives with the hope that the other person will change. This is one of the main reasons why they make excuses for the abuser. They believe that if things get better for the abuser, they will get better overall. This is especially true for people who are experiencing financial hardship or going through a life-altering situation, like an illness, loss of a loved one, or PTSD. Also, because of their love, they feel guilty leaving the other person at their most vulnerable time.

Religion

Victims who are deeply religious will find it hard to leave because it goes against their beliefs and religious values. In religions where separation or revelations of abuse can lead to ostracization, the victim will probably stay in the relationship and may even coerce those around her or him who know about the abuse (like the children) to maintain their silence.

Shared assets

Having children, property, and finances together makes it harder to make the decision to leave. In cases where there are children involved, the abuser may, over time, create a narrative for the children which favors them. The victim is therefore afraid of losing the affection of the children if they leave the relationship. Fear of losing financial stability, especially if the abuser is better off financially, is a major reason why victims stay. In friendships where gaslighting occurs, the victim is afraid of losing the mutual friends they have with the gaslighter. Or, if they live together, this may also be a reason to stay in the abusive friendship.

Empaths are the perfect partners for gaslighters

In the previous chapter, I highlighted the story of Greg, who had a type when it came to the women he chose and on whom his gaslighting tactics always worked. These were women who were trustworthy and empathetic towards others. Such people are known as empaths and their natural disposition makes them a prime target for gaslighters.

Empaths are defined as people with a high sense of awareness of their emotions and those of others around them. They are so in tune with these emotions, that they are keenly aware of others in their space and how they are doing, what they need, and their pain points. Do not confuse empaths with Highly Sensitive People (HSP), who tend to be mainly introverts. Empaths can be either extroverts or introverts. While empaths, like HSP, tend to want a deep and enriching inner life and have a strong desire to help others, they take it further by immersing themselves in the circumstance and experiences of others with the aim of finding ways to help. They will internalize someone else's pain and discomfort, feeling it as closely as their own.

Empaths are the complete opposite of narcissists. On the sensitivity spectrum, narcissists, sociopaths, and psychopaths are at the lowest end of the spectrum, Highly Sensitive People are in the middle section of the spectrum, and empaths are at the highest part of the spectrum. Narcissists are attracted to the nature and disposition of the empath because they exude the confidence, security, and love they so evidently lack. To control such powers and capabilities is alluring for someone who doesn't feel at the same level or at all. This is actually a parasitic relationship, where the abuser feeds off the goodness of their victim, depleting them while inflating their ego in the process.

Empaths need to understand their responses to fear, threats, stress, and uncertainty to be able to develop a healthy way to respond to gaslighting. The typical response of an empath in a gaslighting relationship is to try and fix the situation, rather than leave the abuser. They will try to diminish themselves, thinking that they are focusing on the bigger picture. Because they are so in tune with other people's feelings, they are willing to do all the work to make things work and narcissists use this quality to make them feel guilty when things don't go their way.

It is very important for empaths to understand that their role in the relationship is not to make the narcissist whole and happy. That is the responsibility of the narcissist to themselves. You may be the kindest, most helpful, and most patient person in their lives, but they won't change for you. They can only change for themselves and you have to let them do that. The gift of sensitivity is the first to be exploited by the gaslighter, which is why the victim always wonders, "Am I being too sensitive?"

Empaths embody a few distinct characteristics. Read them below to help you identify if you are one:

You internalize other people's emotions

This is the primary, classic trait of an empath who has the tendency to absorb other people's emotions. This ability to pick up on other people's emotions has long been the subject of debate and, what has emerged, is that people with high levels of empathy have very extremely active mirror neurons. This is the part of the brain which is able to read emotional cues from the people around you, letting you know how they are feeling. This is what makes you discern another person's joy, sadness, anger, or anxiety. Empaths are able to pick up on other people's emotional cues, like darting eyes to show anxiety, a downturn in the mouth, or a change in tone, helping them sense what the other person is feeling.

The depth of their feelings is so strong that catastrophic events seen on TV or heard on the radio can cause them a lot of distress. If they have lived through such an event in their past, this may even incapacitate them. An example of empaths in such situations include those who go to lay flowers, light candles, or hold a vigil at sites of terrorist attacks or other tragedies. These events so move the empaths that they will go to the place where they can feel closest to the victims and their families and make a gesture of love and care.

You go by vibes

The vibe in a room or emanating from other people matters to you. You can make a friend or not, depending on the vibe they emanate. Unfortunately, narcissists are very good at being pretentious and their original vibe can be deceptive. Empaths typically love nature and gardening because they get a sense of peace and are energized in this environment. Conversely, an atmosphere of conflict, chaos, and violence quickly saps an empath's energy and can cause you to become withdrawn.

Going back to the story of Kellie Sutton in chapter one, you will notice that she was described as happy, fun, and vibrant by her friends and family until she got into a relationship with Gane. Her environment caused her to change completely and withdraw so much that it was evident to those who knew her well. Empaths are unable to thrive in foul environments.

You are understanding

This is the reason why people turn to you for advice. You have a level head and have a lot of insight. Because of this, people are drawn to you, including some nasty characters who may want to take advantage of you. Empaths are also excellent listeners because they can put themselves in the other person's shoes and feel their emotions.

You love living things

Empaths love life and living creatures make them happy, so you will find most empaths have a pet, are parents, or are involved in a conservation effort of some kind, either for flora or fauna. Their reactions to either one of the above can seem over the top to other people, but for the empath, these creatures and plants *should* elicit such a reaction. The feelings of an empath are always turned way up compared to other people. It makes sense that empaths are attracted to careers in caregiving, like nursing, elder care, and other healing professions.

You can get easily overwhelmed

As mentioned, the feelings of empaths are highly pronounced, so when they feel both positive and negative emotions, they are susceptible to being overwhelmed. Perhaps this is the primary reason why the gaslighter can eventually tear down the victim's walls of empathy because the empath can feel the anger, irritation, and negative moods emanating from their abuser. This causes them to want to change themselves, conform, accept the alternative truth, and even accept abuse to make the relationship better.

You can detect lies

An empath is able to tell when people are lying because of a liar's subtle emotional cues. So, when an empath is lied to by a gaslighter, they can't easily come to terms with someone who says they love them but is blatantly lying to them. They rationalize the blatant lying by questioning their own reality or perception of events, especially when the gaslighter shifts them in that direction by saying things like, "That is not how I remember it."

You have a calming effect on people

Your voice and demeanor are calming and make the people around you calm down or look at a situation rationally. You will notice that your friends seek you out in moments of turmoil in their lives because they feel you are the level-headed friend. In the same vein, you can't see someone in pain and leave them unhappy. It may be inconvenient for you, but you will be there for your friend until they are fine.

CHAPTER FOUR:

Gaslighting in Intimate Relationships

Life with the charming gaslighter - The horrible truth

Fairytale love stories have given most people a false sense of romance, which is shattered when they begin having relationships and find frogs instead of their Prince Charming. But Alexa is a realist and she has never been that girl waiting for Prince Charming or to be swept off her feet. In fact, when her friends describe her, they all concur that she is a pragmatist, although she is also one of the most caring, loving, helpful, and thoughtful people in their circle of friends.

But when Nicholas came into her life, he seemed hell bent on showing her that the fairytale life existed and he was her Prince Charming. He wined and dined her, flew her to exotic places for holidays, lavished expensive gifts on her, was a gentleman to her, and a sweetheart to her mother. He was her greatest supporter when it came to her career as a cosmetic surgeon. She was pleasantly surprised after a string of cheating men in her life. Her friends were happy for her and her mom was finally thrilled to see her dating and thriving, which made the discrepancies she began to notice right after their wedding hard to share with them.

Since she had her own cosmetic surgery practice, with a small staff and a partner, she could travel with Nicholas during his business meetings all over the world. Plus, he liked having her next to him. He was lost without her and couldn't concentrate when he was away from her. Nicholas was a wealthy man and so he began to drop hints that she didn't need to work. He wanted a family and stability, so he suggested that she quit so that they could start a family.

She refused, of course, and that was the first day she saw the other side of Nicholas. They were having this discussion for the umpteenth time and she was once again explaining why she couldn't give up her career. Suddenly, he hurled his scotch glass across the room and, eyes blazing, turned to her and said, "You are nothing without me! Do you think Tabitha (her partner at the practice) wants you at the clinic? She knows you are not that good and she can do without you!"

Alexa was shocked at first and then she began to feel her anger rising within her. "That is a lie", she said quietly. Tabitha had been her best friend for over 15 years since high school and they had built the practice together from scratch 10 years ago. Nicholas abruptly got off the couch and, changing tactic, let his eyes brim with tears before saying in a hurt tone, "I am only doing this for your own good. I worked hard, so the woman I love can have all the luxuries in life and you continually turn down my loving gesture, like it means nothing to you. Why are you being so cruel to me?" With that, he stormed out of the house and she heard him getting into his car and driving away.

Alexa was unsure of what to feel. She was reeling at his attack, his disparaging manner about her work, and the reference to her best friend, thinking she wasn't good enough. Did Tabitha say something to him? Tabitha didn't like him from the beginning, but seemed to lay off attacking his character after he proposed, so she assumed her friend had come to like her husband eventually. But what was that comment about being cruel to him about? She felt bad that he thought she didn't appreciate the lifestyle he provided for her, but surely she could be appreciative and work at the same time? Sighing, she cleared the broken glass he had thrown across the room and settled on the sofa to wait for him and make things right. He may have overreacted, but he was coming from a place of love.

It was 5 am when Nicholas walked back into the house and, when she woke up to ask him if he was okay and where he had been, he walked right past her. The silent treatment continued for four days and, even when she apologized, he acted like he hadn't heard her. After several days of apologizing and pleading with him, he finally began to talk to her again. But at every turn, he would make a comment about how she should quit her job. The comments ranged from, "Look at how tired you are every day, just because of that practice" to "We could be so much happier if you would only quit your job and spend more time with me." Sometimes, she would find him outside her office waiting for her and he would say that he was lonely in the house without her. He insisted that she travel with him for his business meetings, wherever he went, effectively curtailing the time she spent at her practice. When she mentioned this to him, he replied, "I can see your priority in this relationship is your job and not us. We could be great, but you are ruining it for us by holding on to this job."

Alexa also talked to Tabitha about the comments he had made about her, but Tabitha hadn't even talked to Nicholas in months. In fact, the last time they spoke was the night of Alexa's engagement party, when she congratulated him and Alexa. According to Tabitha, her opinion of Nicholas hadn't changed, but she respected Alexa's decision and their friendship, which is why she backed off.

Six months into the marriage, Nicholas got Alexa a customized, top-of-the-range car, which he parked outside her workplace and waited to surprise her. Alexa walked out of her office laughing with Tim, the head nurse at the clinic and, on seeing her husband, walked over to say hi. Instead of a happy man wishing her a happy birthday and handing her the car keys, he barely smiled at her and tossed her the keys to the car. He hung around to see her friends and colleagues gush over the car and exclaim how lucky she is.

On the way home to prepare for the birthday party he was throwing for her, she was gushing over the car, but he barely said a word. Concerned, she asked him what was wrong and he replied by accusing her of being unfaithful. Shocked by the allegation, she asked him what he was talking about and he asked her who Tim was and how they knew each other. When she replied he was the head nurse at her clinic, he began to call her terrible names, insinuating that they were having an affair and that's why she was not willing to quit her job. Stunned, she sat in her seat quietly the rest of the way home.

They got ready for the party and left together without so much as a word between them. At the party, it was hard for Alexa to act like everything was okay, especially because Tim was there and he was a goofball. When receiving gifts, she could barely meet Tim's eyes and her hug was stiff when he handed her his gift. Mumbling her thanks, she moved on to the next gift, leaving Tim with a frown. She could hear him asking Tabitha if she was ok. She saw her mom and gladly made a beeline for her, giving her a warm hug and offering to take her coat. Her mom quietly said she wanted to see her in private for a minute. Wondering what was the matter, she followed her mother outside. "Hey mom, great to see you. Are you okay?" Her mother was never one for mincing words, so she got straight to the point. "Nicholas says you don't want to have a family. What's going on? I thought this is what you always wanted...a husband...children and a home?" "Unbelievable", Alexa muttered under her breath. "Mom, Nicholas wants me to quit my job and stay at home or travel with him. You know how hard I worked to get that clinic with Tabitha. I can't do that! But I never said I don't want a family. Why must I choose? Why can't I have both?" "He told me you refused to leave the practice and I must say I agree with him. He has everything you need and he is a great provider. He is financially stable for both of you, so why not follow his lead?"

Stunned, Alexa just stared at her mother. The older woman started to fidget under the stare and quickly cleared her throat to add, "Honey, I want you to be happy and you won't get anyone better than Nicholas. He adores you and just wants to make you happy. I think he has a point when he says you are paranoid about your independence. Please reconsider, because he is really hurting about this." Alexa felt deflated and the joy of her birthday flowed out of her. Standing in the warm night air, she started to feel invisible walls closing in.

The drive home was tense and she recalled the look on Tabitha's face when she shared her predicament during the party. Her friend looked horrified, not just at the thought of Alexa quitting the practice, but the support Nicholas was looking for from her mother. When they arrived in the house, Alexa was on the way to the bedroom when a subdued Nicholas called out, "Lexie, sweetheart, I am sorry I accused you and Tim of having an affair. It's just that I can't understand why you are so stubborn about letting me take care of you. Please, just give my proposal a chance and I promise you won't regret it."

"Did you talk to mom about us -- about this?" Alexa asked him. Flinching, he said, "Yes, I did. I was desperate and I thought she could help me talk to you. Your mom knows what I am trying to do here. If I were you, I would listen to her. You know she would never steer you wrong." Alexa could feel the fight draining out of her and she turned to walk away. She went to bed and fell into a disturbed sleep, which was interrupted by loud sobs. Waking up, she is startled to find Nicholas curled up in fetal position at the foot of their bed, loudly sobbing and promising to kill himself if she ever stopped loving him. "Why don't you want to make me happy? Just come and be with me or I swear I will go to the office and not come back one day. Promise me now. Promise you will leave that job and stay with me."

Despite her terror at what she was witnessing, Alexa calmed Nicholas down by placating him and promising she would quit by the end of the month, after she put her affairs in order. He returned to bed and held her tight for the rest of the night, almost like he was holding on to her for dear life. The next day, he seemed to be in a better mood and was more of his loving, jovial self. Alexa began to consider that perhaps she should give up the practice to let peace reign and avoid episodes like the one last night.

Two months later, worn out by the rollercoaster of emotions, Alexa finally quit and sold her share of the practice to Tabitha.

On her last day at work, she could barely stop crying, thinking about what she was giving up. When she got home, she made dinner and informed Nicholas that she was free of her work obligations, just like he wanted. She told him she never wanted him to feel or react the way he did on the night of her birthday party, where he threatened to take his own life over her decisions. Immediately Nicholas responded, "That's not what I said." "Sorry?" said Alexa. "I never said I would take my own life. You must be remembering it wrong. I said that you should promise not to leave me, but I am not suicidal. Maybe that's your thing." said Nicholas.

Alexa sat with a frown on her face, replaying the scene of her birthday, from the car gift to the party and the loud sobbing at night, and she could have sworn he said he would kill himself. That is why she was so worried in the first place and what prompted her to finally take the jump and leave her job. Nicholas was chewing his food and shaking his head saying, "You're crazy. That paranoia of yours is getting out of hand." When she insisted he said those words, he ordered her to stop trying to make him look crazy. He insisted that she was the one acting crazy by accusing him of wanting to kill himself. Alexa let it go, but she kept wondering if he was right.

Over the next three months after she quit her job, Nicholas became withdrawn and when he spoke to her it was an instruction rather than a conversation. He instructed her on what to wear, how to wear her hair, and even whom to talk to. He cut all communication in the house, so she couldn't call out and neither could someone call in. When she asked him why he did this, at first he pretended there was nothing wrong with the phone and she was being paranoid about it. Then, he pretended something was wrong with the phone company and he would sort it out. When she finally followed up with the company and found out their line was not working anymore because he stopped the service, she confronted him and he claimed to have done it for her sake. He knew she was talking to Tabitha every day and it wasn't helping her move on from her previous job and focus on starting a family.

Alexa's mother came by the house for dinner one night and commented about how frail and pale she was looking. "Is everything alright Lexie?" Alexa decided to open up to her mother and explain how Nicholas had changed. He was more controlling and didn't even want her to go grocery shopping alone. "He asked me to stop going to yoga and he even controls what I eat. Tabitha and the girls are not welcome here and Mom, I think I am going crazy because I swear he will say something and later deny ever saying it." As they were speaking, Nicholas walked into the room looking directly at his wife with an icy stare. But, when he turned to his mother-in-law, he gave her a doting, warm smile and a long hug.

"Hey Mom," he said. "You look good." Fixing himself a plate, he said, "Listen, I keep telling you Lexie is paranoid. Now she thinks I don't want her to have any friends. Why would I want that?" Alexa dropped her gaze when he looked at her and then she looked at her mom. Her mother was looking at her strangely and abruptly she asked her to help her serve the dessert she had brought for dinner. In the kitchen, Alexa's mother asked her directly, "Has Nicholas ever hit you?" "Nooo mom, it's not physical it's just...I can't explain it." said Alexa.

"Well, maybe you are just reading a lot more into his actions than you should, now that you are at home more. Like he said...why would he prevent you from seeing your friends? This is marriage, honey. You guys just need to understand each other."

Alexa tried to understand her husband, but the more she tried, the more she made no sense of his behavior. Two years into the marriage, they still didn't have children because Nicholas said he wanted everything to be perfect. When she questioned him about it, he would say, "We can get pregnant right now if you want, but with your paranoia, I don't think you would make a good mom." On his birthday, he sulked and when she asked him why he was mad, he complained about her present. "You give me the cheapest presents, which tells me you don't love me as much as I love you. If you did, you would invest in me and my happiness. We could be great together, but you just keep messing things up."

He no longer took her on his business trips because she didn't behave and was an embarrassment to him. One time during a dinner with some of his business partners, she engaged in conversation with an important member of the business delegation and he complimented Nicholas on having such an intelligent and charming wife. Immediately, he pulled her aside and told her to stop showing him up. On the way home, he exploded, saying, "This is exactly why I don't take you anywhere anymore. You just have to make a spectacle of yourself and make me look bad. You think he thought you were smart? He was just being polite. I can't have kids with someone like you." Alexa was now used to these outbursts, so she didn't flinch. Instead, she promised to be a better, quiet wife. At home, she wearily got out her clothes and into her pajamas, thinking to herself that she was so weary and alone.

The next day, she informed her husband that she needed to go and get a haircut. It was one of the things that she looked forward to, although he had started insisting that her hairdresser come to the house. At the hair salon, she bumped into Tabitha, whom she hadn't seen in close to 10 months. On seeing her friend, the tears started to stream down her face. Tabitha was shocked at how beaten her friend looked. She insisted on having a long lunch. While pushing her food around on her plate, Alexa told her friend everything that had been going on. Because Nicholas had taken away her phone and given her a phone with just his number and a few of his friend's numbers, she couldn't get in touch with anyone.

Alexa said she was afraid she was losing her mind, amid heart-wrenching sobs. Tabitha went across the street and bought her a phone and gave it to her to hide. "If you need me for anything, call me and I will come over, no matter what time of the day. Keep this safe, Alexa, this is your lifeline." They returned to the salon and had their hair done and, during that time, Tabitha could see fleeting glimpses of her vibrant friend when she smiled. "Why do you hide your smile behind your hand? You never used to do that," asked Tabitha. The veil of sadness immediately descended on her friend's face. "Nicholas doesn't like my smile because of my crooked teeth." What crooked teeth? Your teeth are perfect -- they always have been." At that moment, Tabitha realized what her friend was going through. She was being gaslit and she didn't even realize it! If she didn't do something, Alexa's life would be destroyed. But what can she do?

As they parted ways, Tabitha said a short prayer for her friend to be safe.

On arriving home, Alexa was confronted by a furious Nicholas. "I called the salon to talk to you since you conveniently left your phone behind and they said you had left with another woman. Who is she? Or is she a decoy for you to meet your lover? I knew you were not worth anything and that's why I can't have kids with you." Alexa tried to explain that it was Tabitha. "Ohhhh Tabitha! Was she picking you up so you could go and see Tim?" Alexa was so exhausted and drained, she just broke down in tears and let him continue to rant and hurl abuses at her. When it got too much, she ran into the bathroom and locked herself inside. She was just starting to compose herself when she heard the sound of an electrical appliance at the door. Not sure what was going on, she decided to wash her face before emerging. Suddenly, she saw the door teetering on its hinges. He was taking the door off at the hinges to get to her! She was terrified watching the door be dismantled and was sure she would die there today if he got to her. Instead, he calmly placed the door to the side after removing it and said to her, "I don't want there to be any barriers between us. This is me showing you that I love you."

That night, she sank into sleep, still disturbed by the events of the day, only to be woken up by the sound of glass shattering. She thought it was a burglar, so she reached out for Nicholas but he wasn't in bed. Tiptoeing downstairs, she whispered loudly, "Nicholas!" Then, she noticed the study door was open. She ran to it and found Nicholas lying in a heap, a glass of scotch shattered nearby and pills on his table and floor. She screamed and called 911. This was the third time he had done this. Nicholas was rushed to the hospital and his stomach pumped. When she went to visit him he looked at her sullenly and said, "Look what you made me do. I can't lose you. And if there is someone else, I won't ever let you be happy. If I can't have you, I won't let you have peace without me, even if it means I have to die and come back to haunt you."

As Alexa stood there looking at him, it struck her how much helplessness had overcome her. The nurse walked in and informed her that visiting hours are over. She leaned over him and kissed his forehead. "See you, Nicholas." "Come earlier tomorrow, so we can spend more time together," he said. As she walked out, she reached for a phone in her bag and dialed the only number in it. "Tabitha, please come and help me pack my stuff."

Alexa got a restraining order against Nicholas and filed for divorce. She relocated somewhere where Nicholas couldn't trace her, using the money from selling Tabitha her part of the clinic. Last she heard, Nicholas was on trial for domestic violence. Looking back on the three years she gave the man, she wondered what would have happened if she hadn't walked away. Would she be alive or dead? Thank god, she didn't have to find out. Alexa's mom walked up to Nicholas one day in the parking lot of a local grocery store and gave him a resounding slap on the face. "That is for breaking the most precious thing in my life."

7 stages of gaslighting in a relationship

Gaslighting is a persistent form of abuse that doesn't let up and is gradually done to the victim. When experienced in a mild form, there is a subtle shift in power in which the victim is always subjugated to the abuser.

When one experiences severe gaslighting, they can become completely disoriented from reality and be completely mind-controlled by the abuser. Cult leaders are known for employing severe gaslighting, which involves heavy mind control tactics to get their members to commit tragic acts, like killing themselves or even killing others, like in the case of the Charles Manson and the Manson family.

There are seven stages to gaslighting. Each builds on the previous and takes the level of manipulation up a notch higher.

Step 1: Exaggerate and lie

I have established that gaslighting is built on a foundation of lies. Like I said, without lies it is impossible to execute gaslighting. But to be effective in gaslighting, the lie needs a little exaggeration. The exaggeration is meant to establish different facts that mesmerize the victim into feeling that the story has too many details to be a lie. The better the embellishment, the more believable the story.

Gaslighters are masters at embellishing and spinning a new narrative around a story. For example, perhaps you both ran into one of your friends of the opposite gender and the interaction was public, but afterward, the gaslighter will introduce embellishments of how the interaction went, in order to support his or her narrative. If it was a friend who touched your shoulder while speaking to you, the gaslighter will declare that they were flirting with you and you didn't notice, but he or she can tell what the friend was trying to do. A simple, innocent meeting will go from being a fun interaction to something nefarious, supported by the exaggeration of the gaslighter. The victim is left wondering if there was something they missed and thanking the gaslighter for looking out their wellbeing.

They will also lie about you to other people in a bid to discredit you. For example, a gaslighting boss will lie about your performance and even blame you for mistakes made in the company, even when you have nothing to do with the responsible department. Facts and evidence may prove otherwise, but that doesn't mean they won't try to frame you, just to discredit you.

The lies are meant to breakdown the truth threshold of the victim and put the victim on the defensive. During this stage, you can expect to hear phrases like:

"Your department is a waste of resources because you don't get anything done. How do you justify your salary?"

"You wouldn't know the truth if it smacked you in the face. You can't remember even the most basic details of information, so I have to keep steering you right."

Step 2: Repetition

Donald Trump is known as the "Gaslighter in Chief" and one of his favorite tactics is the repetition of falsehoods until his base and others begin to believe his words to be true. For example, during one of his rallies, he pointed to the members of the press who were covering the event and called them "fake news". The crowd began to boo the press. The President of the United States called the media fake news, which his base believes. Formerly well-respected media houses, like CNN and BBC, have lost credibility with some members of the public.

But are these media houses really fake news? From their coverage, there is plenty of proof that their news is fact-checked and their sources are credible. In fact, media houses like CNN have fact-checked the president on some of his blatant lies and exaggerations proving the fake news source is in fact Donald Trump. But he has repeated the phrase so many times and used it to discredit credible sources of news and in the process established a pattern that is now used by dictators around the world. Dictators now call any unfavorable news fake news.

This is the perfect example of what happens when gaslighters repeat certain phrases. They become the alternative to the truth, but they are accepted by many as the real truth. In intimate relationships, the gaslighter uses words like "crazy", "paranoid", "sick", "unstable", and "insane" to describe their victim in public and this can cause friends, family, and even acquaintances to look at the "gaslightee" through those lenses.

The repetition of lies gives the gaslighter dominance over the conversation and keeps the victim on the constant defensive, which makes them appear unstable, even to themselves. Some victims will withdraw from conversations completely, in order to avoid being portrayed by their partner in this way, but the abuser will still use their silence to show how their condition is deteriorating. You can't win with a gaslighter.

Step 3: Escalation

Escalation typically occurs in a gaslighting relationship when the gaslighter is challenged, causing them to raise the bar. This is when one notices the gaslighter either getting violent, aggressive, or threatening to people around them. He or she will focus on people the victim values the most, like their children or elderly parents, threatening to cause harm to them or take the kids away.

Calling out a gaslighter on their lies makes them feel vulnerable and this causes them to want to regain dominance. To do this, they have to find something that will double down on the control over the victim, so they focus on things the victim loves. You can expect to hear phrases like:

"You know, this paranoia is why I think the kids are in danger around you. Who knows what you will say to them. I will take the kids away from you because you are a danger to them." Or,

"Your parents are better off without you since you are just becoming crazier and crazier. I will put them in a home and make sure you never cause them distress like this again. They also know you are crazy. Imagine what this is doing to them. You are a horrible daughter/son."

Remember that gaslighters do not play fair, so they have no shame using underhanded tactics on their victims. The escalation is meant to put fear into the victim and let them know they have no recourse for their situation. It creates a feeling of helplessness and constant anxiety. This is one of the reasons a victim stays in the relationship for years. They honestly believe they are protecting their loved ones by staying with the gaslighter and obeying him. Don't rock the boat and everything will be okay.

They may also get aggressive and abusive in the actions towards the victim. Physical abuse is not uncommon in gaslighting relationships.

Step 4: Wear out the victim

Wearing out the victim is a real strategy used by gaslighters. In the story of Alex and Nicholas, the latter constantly complained about his wife working and even used his mother in law to "talk some sense" into his wife. When she remained adamant, he threatened to kill himself, gave her the silent treatment, and emotionally blackmailed her into submission.

By constantly being on the offensive, the gaslighter keeps his or her victim on the defensive, which can be an exhausting state to be in, especially with someone you love. The fighting fatigue soon sets in and the victim doesn't want to be at constant odds with the other person.

The gaslighter can also wear out the victim by constantly attacking their responses to situations or their perception of events. Eventually, the victim begins to accept the narrative of their abusers because they become resigned to their fate and are filled with pessimism about the future. You must remember that the goal of the gaslighter is to break their victim and grind them into the ground, which will only happen by wearing them out with negativity.

Stage 5: Encourage a codependent relationship

The gaslighter needs their victim to become dependent on them, so they foster a relationship in which the victim looks to the abuser for verification of the reality she or he is experiencing. To create a codependent relationship, the abuser creates situations of constant insecurity, uncertainty, and anxiety in their victim. They dangle certain things in front of their victim, like starting a family, love, security, or even financial security, which puts the victim on strings to be played like a puppet any time the abuser feels like it. You will hear phrases like the following in this stage:

"I see that you are trying to behave, so I won't take the kids away from you. But you must promise me that you will be good because you know I have the power to take them from you."

"I have told you that your friends are just jealous of us. See how they want to make plans on the day I have planned our date night. You are better off without friends like that. Just you and me babe, we are enough for each other. We don't need anyone else."

For the codependency to take root, the victim must be marginalized from people who could show him or her the real definition of love and care. Exposing the victim to people who love them is counterproductive to what the gaslighter is trying to achieve. The victim must be made to believe that the abuser is the only person who has their best interests at heart. The codependent relationship is built on fear and lies and it allows the abuser to be the dominant partner in the relationship.

The gaslighter loves to play savior to the victim in the relationship, making the other person feel like they are the only safe place the victim has. Any codependent relationship is fraught with doubt and anxiety, not to mention confusion, and this one is no different. Unfortunately, only one person in the relationship feels this way.

Stage 6: False hope

This is the time that the manipulation is in full play. The gaslighter creates a scenario where they give the victim a sense of false hope that things will go back to the original love they shared or the stability that existed in the initial stages of their relationship. The false hope stage includes treating the victim with kindness and acting like the abuser really cares. Intimate dinners, gifts, and even gentle treatment is laid on thick for the benefit of the victim. But, just as suddenly as the kindness and romance came back, it will abruptly be withdrawn.

You see, the abuser gives false hope to throw the victim off-kilter and also to remind them that, just as easily as they can be loved, they can be discarded. During the period of false hope, which can last a day to a couple of days or maybe even a week, the abuser builds up the victim with the sole intention of tearing them down in such a destructive manner that they will be incapacitated by the letdown.

This is perhaps one of the most toxic parts of gaslighting, as the abuser intentionally inflicts psychological torture and torment. Not only do they know what they are doing in building false hope, but they try to make the victim feel guilty when they tear them down. At this stage, you will hear phrases like:

"Look at what you have done. It's your fault we are not happy. You see how hard I am trying to make us work and then you just go and try to show me up in public."

"What is wrong with you? Why can't you get what I am trying to do for us? If this doesn't work out, it is all your fault because God knows, I try."

"Why are you dressed like that? Do you expect me to go out with you looking like that? That's it. You clearly don't appreciate what I am trying to do here for you, so just go back upstairs and change. We aren't going out anymore."

Any cries by the victim to rectify the situation fall on deaf ears and the abuser is back in control, while the victim is left blaming themselves for ruining their chance at getting back their original love.

This tactic is used by the gaslighter anytime he or she sees the victim either unresponsive to their mind control game or showing some signs of resistance to the abuser's behavior. It is a very effective tactic in reminding the victim of who is the boss.

Step 7: Dominance

The ultimate goal of the gaslighter is to gain dominance and control over the victim. They do so in order to take advantage of the other person and, in some cases, have access to their valuables.

Dominance is achieved by having a constant and consistent flow of lies and mind games, including coercion. The abuser strives to keep the victim in a constant state of fear and doubt, which is why they will isolate them from their friends and family, who could give them perspective and reinforce their sanity. Dominance allows the abuser to exploit the victim at will and without any repercussions.

The love bombing tactic

Love bombing involves the gaslighter using over the top shows of affection to the victim in a bid to emotionally manipulate them. Besides the Intimidator Gaslighter, the Glamour Gaslighter and the Nice Guy Gaslighter typically use this tactic. It happens early in the relationship, in which the gaslighter manipulates the response of the victim by buying lavish gifts and taking him or her to expensive places for dinner or on vacation. There are signs that you are being love-bombed early in the relationship, including:

Saying what you want to hear

All of us have insecurities and when we share them with a love bombing expert, like a gaslighter, they will consistently say what they think you want to hear in order to inflate your ego or gain your affection. For example, maybe you hate the way your nose looks (we all have parts of our body that we don't like). The gaslighter will constantly tell you your nose is their favorite part of your body and, no, it doesn't look hawkish -- it looks regal. There is no genuine honesty in their compliment, instead, they serve the purpose of manipulating you.

Claiming you could do better

Beware of the partner who constantly tells you that you could do better because there is underlying insecurity in them. In the case of a gaslighter, they are trying to gain your sympathy and want to seem like they feel privileged and humbled that you chose them. Deep down, this is a manipulation tactic.

They might also begin to criticize your friends, career choice, colleagues, and even family members, saying you could do better. This is a ploy to ensure isolation from the people who love you, in order to enhance their manipulation. If your partner, early on in the relationship, starts suggesting that your friends or family don't have your best interest at heart but he/she does, they are trying to separate you from your support system. These claims are usually followed by a lavish gift or an expensive getaway, to make them look like they care about you.

They give expensive gifts

Now, receiving expensive gifts from a potential partner early on in a relationship is not a red flag in itself. But there are telltale signs that it is a love bombing tactic, especially if the giver makes a point to tell you how much the gift cost. Not only are they trying to impress you, they want to make you feel guilty when they don't get their way. After all, they spent all that money on you and all they ask for is just your love and affection.

For the gaslighter, telling you how much they spent on you is their process of quantifying their investment in you and estimating your value as a person.

They lavish compliments

Gaslighters know that their victims want compliments. Remember, they know what you want to hear and they use compliments to condition you. Their complements are used to manipulate you into being what they need you to be. With time, their compliments shape you. For example, if the gaslighter tells you that you look good in black dresses, you will probably start wearing more black dresses in order to always look great to him. If they say you don't need makeup because your skin is flawless, you will probably stop using makeup in a bid to make them happy. This is conditioning you to make you the person they want to have in the future.

Public displays of affection

During the love bombing stage, the gaslighter loves public displays of affection. They will touch you, kiss you, and show warm body language in front of your loved ones. This is to prove to everyone that you guys are good together and he or she is into you. It sets you up to look like the offending party when you try to pull away from the person. Most victims are also taken in by the PDA and will believe it comes from a genuine place.

In return, they will expect you to return the affection by being obedient and listening to what they say. When they want to see you, they expect you to drop everything and show up. If you are unavailable, they take that as a rejection and typically have an extreme reaction to this. This introduces a pattern of extreme reactions, unmanageable expectations, and that walking on eggshells feeling.

CHAPTER FIVE:

Gaslighting in the Family

When parents are gaslighters, lives are lost

Suzie and her mother were close. They always had popcorn dates together when she was a kid and watched their favorite movies. They talked about the boys she liked as a teenager and talked on the phone every day of the week when she went to college. Her mom was a single parent and she was warm, fun, friendly, and beautiful. She also never spoke to her own mom, who was living in a different neighborhood but in the same city.

Growing up, Suzie's mother refused to take phone calls from her grandmother and Suzie only met and talked to the elderly woman twice or thrice in her life. She found out that her mother had a brother who passed away as a teenager from suicide. As she grew older, she found out that her mother blamed her grandmother for his death. During dinner at her mom's house one day, she broached the subject of her grandmother, asking about her and why her mom never spoke about her.

"I knew this day would come," said Suzie's mom. "Grab that bottle of wine and meet me in the den. I'll go get some pictures. It's time you met your uncle and your grandmother." In the den, Suzie's mom looked at a picture of a young man who looked like her and was holding her hand. In the picture, Suzie's mom was grinning at the young man, who looked down on her beaming. "This is your uncle, Tyler. He was so smart and kind and funny. Next to you, he was my favorite person in the whole world. He killed himself when I was 13 years old." This was the first time Suzie's mom had spoken about how her brother died.

"My mom was a pathological liar and mean as a rattlesnake and Tyler was her victim of choice. He was too sensitive and she destroyed him day by day until he couldn't take it anymore. She would lie to him about everything and lie about him, as well. She told him his girlfriend was cheating on him with his best friend and when he confronted the girl, he found out it wasn't true. They broke up and when my brother confronted my mom, she pretended she didn't say that and he must have heard her wrong. She always told him that he only needed her."

"My brother mentioned this to our grandfather, who asked mom. My mother said that my brother made up the whole cheating situation and is now blaming her. She said this in brother's presence and even added, 'You know how he is.' "One day we were grocery shopping and my mom slipped some eyeliner into my brother's backpack. He was arrested by the store security and my mother accused him of stealing it for one of his girlfriends. My brother denied it and she refused to get him out of jail that night, saying he needed to learn his lesson. I know it was her because I saw her do it, but I was too scared to tell anyone. My grandfather heard about the incident and asked my brother about it. My mom chimed in to the conversation, saying my brother was a liar and again adding, 'You know how he is."

Before long, my grandfather began to regard my brother as a troublemaker and my brother was so confused by what was happening, he began to withdraw into himself. There were many times when my mom called my brother names, like a liar, thief, good for nothing, dumb...the list was endless. My brother stopped hanging out with his friends because she would call his friends' parents and tell them he was a bad influence and was doing drugs and stealing. No one at school would come near my brother and he started to get bullied, really badly. He never told my mom about it, although he tried to tell my grandfather. Grandpa called mom and told her to go to school and find out what was happening. My mom told him not to bother because my brother was just looking for attention.

Two weeks later my brother slashed his wrists in the school bathroom. In his bag was a collection of notes from one of the school bullies telling him to kill himself. The note said that no one wanted him, not even his own mother. My brother never understood why mom hated him so much. My mother lost custody of me to my dad who took care of me and I haven't spoken to her since my brother was buried. She cried at my brother's funeral, vowing to find out what happened to her boy. But it was all for show. I never let you near her because she is a master gaslighter. I am grateful that I went to live with my dad because I think she would have done the same thing to me."

The toxic things that gaslighting parents can do

They dictate your likes and dislikes

This means that they tell the child what she or he likes or doesn't like. They say things like, "What do you mean you don't like baseball?" Or, "We are a family of meat-eaters. There is no place for vegetarians in this house." As a result, they force their preferences on the child.

They dismiss your feelings

"Stop crying!" Or, "Don't cry like a baby because you got hit during a game!" These are some of the phrases that parents use to dismiss sad or unhappy feelings. This conditions the child not to feel or show emotion, even when they are hurting. Eventually, the child learns to take their hurt out on something or someone else.

They minimize your achievements

Toxic families are characterized by bullying tactics in which the victim is downtrodden and their achievements are not validated. For example, if the child is great academically, the father might say, "Books don't matter in this world if you don't know how to take care of yourself." Or, "I don't care about straight As -- if you can't play ball, you are not a man." They will also make fun of your achievements, calling them silly and time-wasting.

They will label you

You might be called silly or paranoid or that you have a wild imagination. These labels are easy to put on kids because children are known to have imaginary friends or play most of the time. But in a gaslighting situation at home, it is meant to cast doubt on the child's reality.

If the child calls the gaslighter out on their behavior, the parent will label them rude, undisciplined, or a troublemaker, in order to make themselves feel better.

Gaslighting children

Gaslighting is a common occurrence in dysfunctional families and the gaslighter is typically the mother or the father of the child. Gaslighting is insidious in nature to anyone, but in children, it is especially devastating because the cycle of emotional abuse can continue even into adulthood. The children will also tend to choose gaslighters for their life partners.

The children stuck with gaslighting parents typically lose their confidence and they tend to have little to no integrity, through no fault of their own. When the child perceives the parent as the enemy, it is particularly traumatizing.

4 types of gaslighting in childhood and their effects

Even the most well-meaning parent can be a gaslighter without knowing it. If you give your child conflicting information that conscientiously contradicts the reality they saw, you have gaslit them. For example, your daughter or son walks in on you having a piece of chocolate and you have been saying all week that you are on a diet and are off sweets. When they ask you what you are eating and you say nothing after hurriedly swallowing the chocolate, you have gaslit your child.

Some parents like to call them white lies, but they are dangerous because they set up a precedent of alternative realities. If you do this frequently, your child can become conditioned to a skewed sense of perception.

Four types of childhood gaslighting

Double-bind gaslighting

This type of gaslighting parent was first identified in 1965 and it has been linked to schizophrenia and a personality disorder. The perfect example of double-bind gaslighting is when the parent tells the child they love them and can even be smothering in their love sometimes and, the next minute, the parent coldly rejects the child or inflicts corporal punishment.

The message is very confusing for the child, who feels loved one minute and unwanted the next. The effect of such gaslighting is that the child grows up unsure of their validity and they always question what others say to them. Questions like, "Am I worthy or not?" always plague them, especially in relationships, from life partners and friends to even at work.

Appearance focused gaslighting

In this type of gaslighting, the child is expected to uphold the status of the family by putting up appearances that everything is perfect, even when it is not. You will find that victims of sexual abuse by a family member have been gaslit in this way. Achievement focused parents also tend to engage in this type of gaslighting.

This type of gaslighting makes it difficult for the child to accept human weakness in themselves and others, as they grow up. It also makes it difficult to let other people in because of the fear of being vulnerable. The message in appearance focused gaslighting is that we must appear perfect and what happens in the family stays in the family. Your pain and reality don't matter.

Unpredictable gaslighting

In this type of gaslighting, the child is not sure how the parent will react to a situation. The same mistake is met by uncontrollable rage in some cases and, at other times, the parent is lucid and even gentle and understanding. Parents who are manic depressive or have a history of substance abuse are most likely to engage in this type of gaslighting.

The message to the child in this type of gaslighting is that you can never be stable. Anything can happen to you at any time. As a result, the child is not able to read people's characters and intentions as they grow older. This puts them at the risk of ending up with a similar abuser as a life partner.

Emotional negligence gaslighting

This type of gaslighting involves emotionally neglecting the child, although their physical needs are met. The parent will attack the child for showing emotion most of the time, saying things like "Don't you dare cry", "Suck it up" or, "I have no time for sensitive people."

The message to the child is that their emotions are irrelevant and they are not to be shared with anyone else. Such kids grow up feeling that they are lacking in a certain aspect of themselves and will seek people, like gaslighters, who will fulfill that side of them.

CHAPTER SIX:

Gaslighting in the Workplace

How working with a gaslighter nearly derailed a career

Macy had been working at one of the premier hotels in Dubai for over two years as a front office agent. Her work was exceptional and professional, which was proven by the guest interactions and accolades from the hotel brass. At the beginning of her third year in the same role, a new hotel manager was employed. The female boss took an instant dislike to Macy and, from their first interaction, was curt and short with her.

Thinking she may have done something to offend her, Macy set out to make things right. She asked for a sit-down and broached the subject by asking if there was anything the new manager had seen about her work that she felt Macy should improve. The manager launched into a litany of things she noticed about Macy that she should change, but none of them were based on her work, rather they were personal issues. "I don't like the way you wear your hair. Are you a natural blonde?" "Yes, I am" "Are you sure? Because it looks like you have bleached your hair. I have nothing against blondes. It's just that you look like you are trying to stand out and be noticed more. I think that is unprofessional." "I assure you that I am a natural blonde and my hair color is not a ploy to attract more attention to myself," said Macy. "Are you married?" asked the manager. "Not yet," replied Macy. "Mmmhhhh." said the manager, as if it all made sense now. With that, Macy was dismissed. She left wondering whether her hair color attracted more attention and if she looked like that's what she was trying to do.

About three weeks later, a colleague in the accounts office stopped Macy in the corridor to ask her what was wrong with her paperwork. "Nothing, as far as I know," replied Macy. "Why do you ask?" "Well, the hotel manager asked for all your paperwork dating back six months," said the colleague. "Why?" asked Macy. "I don't know why but she asked specifically for your paperwork and no one else's," said the other employee. That afternoon, she was summoned to the manager's office to find her paperwork neatly placed in a pile next to the manager.

I have been going through your work and I must say I am shocked you have lasted this long here," she began. Your paperwork is sloppy, you haven't attached supporting guest payment slips, and I don't see the relevant signatures on the credit card slips. How do you justify your salary? Do you think you are here to just look good?" Stunned, Macy finally found her voice to say "Sorry, I am confused here a little. No one in the accounts department raised any questions with me, so I am not sure what I have failed to do here. May I please see an example of the incomplete paperwork?" "Do you think I am making this up?" asked the manager. "I have tons of proof here. The accounts department also doesn't think you are competent. They all concur with me that your work is shoddy. I am putting you on six-month probation as I review your work. And, may I suggest that you consider a darker color for your hair so you are less conspicuous."

Macy stumbled out of the manager's office and went to the ladies' room to wash her face. "What is going on," she asked herself. She has been at the front desk for longer than anyone and her work has always been praiseworthy. Did the accounts department really believe her work was shoddy? Why didn't anyone say something? Maybe she had become complacent and wasn't giving her very best these days. She would make sure her work was impeccable.

For the next few months, she endured constant criticism, comparison, and even subtle bullying by the manager. So when a position opened up in another branch, she applied just to get out from under the thumb of her current boss. The manager heard about it and called the recruiting officer to "caution" him against offering the position to Macy. But since Macy was one of the last interviewees left standing, the recruiting officer scheduled a final interview with her nonetheless. Macy emerged as the best candidate, so the recruiter decided to have a candid conversation with her about her "reputation."

Macy, I am very impressed. You clearly are the best person for the job, but I have some concerns. To begin with, your boss got in touch with me and raised some concerns about your work. So, I asked the accounting office to share your paperwork with me and I honestly didn't find anything wrong with your work. A few mistakes here and there, but nothing that seems as major as your hotel manager tried to imply. Tell me about your relationship with the hotel manager at your branch." Macy decided to be honest with the recruiter about the relationship with her boss.

"I am certainly not surprised to hear this. This manager has become a notorious gaslighter, especially with female staff whom she feels threatened by. I would like to offer you the job and I would also like you to share your experience with the human resources director." It turned out that this manager had been gaslighting employees for years and most people were too afraid to lose their jobs to report her actions. The recruiter was one of her victims and she had decided enough is enough.

How to identify gaslighting at work

Gaslighting at work can be subtler because the abuser is more aware of their surroundings. He or she is usually a point of authority or a peer to the abuser, but junior staff can also be excellent gaslighters, especially if they are ambitious and eying a job opening with stiff competition. You can tell you are being gaslighted at work when you see telltale signs like:

- The gaslighter is spreading misinformation about you.
- You are the subject of gossip and blatant lies spread by one specific person.
- The gaslighter is very charming and witty around you.

- They try to get your contribution and then twist your words and use them against you.
- The gaslighter discredits you, leaving you feeling like you are not worthy.
- They make passive-aggressive comments about you under the guise of jokes or being friendly.

How common gaslighting tactics are used at work

Countering

This tactic involves the gaslighter questioning your memory of events, especially those that happened when you are together. For example, if you shared clients and were in a meeting together, they may question your notes and imply that what you wrote was inaccurate, only to write a report with the same version of events. When confronted, they will blatantly deny ever having changed the version of events, claiming you misunderstood what they said.

Withholding

The colleague or superior withholds pertinent information to your work, making it impossible for you to be effective at your job. They also withhold praise, even where it is due, with phrases like "That is what you are paid to do. There is nothing special about what you achieve."

Trivializing

If you close a deal or get a promotion, they find a way to trivialize the achievement. They may say "That is a minor achievement. At your age, I was on the fast track to becoming the company managing director." This leads the victim to think their ideas and input or achievements are not important.

Lying

Gaslighters at work will lie in order to paint their victim in a bad light. This works to their advantage because it casts doubt on their victim's competence. It also launches the victim into a state of anxiety and self-doubt.

Diverting

The gaslighter will divert attention from the subject of work to focus on the victim's emotional or private life. For example, Macy's manager shifted focus from the aim of the meeting, which was Macy looking for feedback about her work, to criticizing Macy's looks and style.

Phrases gaslighters use in the workplace

The following are common in a gaslighting work-related relationship:

- You need to concentrate.
- Don't you remember us discussing this yesterday?
- I always have to repeat myself because you can't remember stuff.
- If you could just learn how to listen, we wouldn't have this problem.
- You are being too sensitive.
- Stop being paranoid/irrational.
- You are too emotional.
- You read too much in my comments -- I am just trying to help.
- Can you hear what you just said? What does that say about you?
- Are you going through something at home? You are always behind on things.
- I only have these sorts of problems with you.
- You need to learn to take a joke. You are too thin-skinned.
- I am always reminding you of things because you have poor organization.
- I am hard on you because I like you.

The gaslighting boss and their tactics

They bad-mouth you

The gaslighting boss will find ways to bad-mouth you to other senior-level members of the company and your peers. This is a tactic to make you lose credibility with other members of the company, so when you make complaints, you don't have a friendly ear or support. They will also blatantly lie about you.

They move deadlines

A boss who gaslights their juniors makes unreasonable demands on them that he or she knows will cast the employee(s) in a bad light. For example, they will move a deadline up, knowing it will be impossible to produce the work within the new timeframe. And if asked why they moved the deadline, they may deny ever moving it.

They make insulting comments

This tactic falls under the diverting gaslighting technique. They will say something underhanded, like making a racist comment disguised as a joke. If you call them out about it, they will claim you are being too sensitive. They will say it in front of people and, when they face backlash, they will claim you misunderstood the comment or that everyone says it.

They exclude you

You are the one person missing the important team emails by accident, which impacts how you do your work. On the extreme end, the boss may even take credit for your ideas or work and exclude you from getting credit for your work. When you confront them, they will say there is no solo effort and it's always a team effort.

CHAPTER SEVEN:

Gaslighting in Friendships

A toxic friendship hidden in plain sight

Mike and Sam had been friends since they were in junior high. Every day after school, they would hang out in Mike's treehouse for hours on end, doing their homework, playing video games, and checkers. They were there for each other's first kisses and they talked about all their crushes. Nothing could separate them.

They applied to different colleges and so came their separation. Although the two friends visited each other, their visits became far and few in between. Three years after graduation, the two friends found themselves in the same city and bumped into each other during a morning coffee run. Mike thought the person ahead of him in the queue sounded familiar, so he stuck his head out from the back of the queue to see if it was who he thought it was. Sure enough, it was Sam.

Mike left the queue and followed his childhood friend as he walked out of the coffee shop, wrapping his arms tight around him and growling, "Give me your coffee, nice and slow." Alarmed, Sam turned around ready to punch his would-be assailant, but was instead met with the wide grin of his friend. "Ohhh...Mikey! Oh my God! What...How long has it been?" "Too long, my brother! I haven't seen you in over five years. How are you?" replied Mike. "I'm good, man - just grabbing my morning coffee on the way to work. I have a small tech startup, developing medical apps to help patients reach caregivers faster. How is your practice?" said Sam.

"You know the law. Everybody hates lawyers, but they sure love to keep us busy. How is Charlene and the kids?" asked Mike. "Everyone is fine. We would love to have you over for dinner. As a matter of fact, come over this Saturday, I am sure Charlene won't mind me making plans." Replied Sam, "That sounds great! Here is my business card. If you guys change your mind, let me know" said Mike.

The two friends rekindled their friendship and started hanging out more often. During their hangouts, Mike would always make underhanded jokes about Sam's race and his struggle with weight loss. It began with phrases like, "Put the fork down, otherwise you will go back to being known as 'Sam the Bubble.'" This was despite the fact that Sam was lean and fit as a whip. In fact, Mike was the chubbier of the two, but his references were to the bullying and teasing Sam experienced in junior high because of his weight.

During one of their conversations, he said, "You know your wife is a real mammy. She loves to take care of other people and makes a great presence in the house." Shocked, Sam looked at his friend and asked him, "What did you just say?" "You know, she has that nurturing character that is inherent in black women. I am sure she takes excellent care of you. Just look at you. It's a compliment bro! You know I am saying this because I love Charlene," replied Mike. For the rest of the evening, Sam was subdued and when he saw his friend off, his hug was lackluster. Should he tell Charlene what Mike said? She would lose her mind and confront him. Maybe Mike was just paying a compliment the best way he knew how, but why use a slavemaster's slang. He had known Mike all his life and the man didn't have an evil bone in his body. He choked it down to ignorance on his friend's part and decided that the next time they hung out, he would educate him.

The two friends played golf often and, on the days they played together, Mike had a nasty habit of counting the number of black people versus the number of white people on the course. "More and more black people are playing golf these days, I guess. After Tiger Woods, all of you thought you could do it. But you know, the only reason he even got in through the door was because he had a white, blonde wife. That is every black man's come up."

"What the hell are you talking about?" exploded Sam. "First, Tiger Woods is the greatest of all-time in golf. Second, my people don't need a 'come up' from any white man or woman. What has come over you with these racist comments?" Walking away from Mike, Sam replaced his club back in the bag, heaved it on to his shoulder and started off towards the golf cart. Mike caught up with Sam and said, "Why are you being so sensitive? I don't mean you. I respect you and I thought I could be myself around you. Why are you being emotional about this? We are friends and we can speak freely around each other. You are acting crazy."

The ride off the course was terse and the two men parted ways without saying anything. When Sam got home, his wife asked him what had transpired between him and Mike. "How did you know something happened?" he asked. "Well, Mike called me to tell me that you were acting funny, paranoid even. That you went off at him about him praising Tiger Woods and commenting about seeing more black people on the course, which he thought was great," Charlene explained. Sam let out a loud sigh and asked his wife to sit down. "Mike has been making some very disturbing comments about black people. He disparages me about my weight and, when I confront him about it, he says I am overreacting, being too sensitive, or that I am crazy. I know what he is saying and it's not right."

"I didn't want to tell you this, but Mike came over to my workplace the other day and he claimed he was worried about how you are behaving. He said you have been looking at other women when you two are together and even approached one woman to ask her for her number. He asked me not to tell you, so he could find proof for me. I didn't tell you because I was honestly shocked and it's been two days of me thinking about what to do with this information. But from what you have told me, I think Mike is gaslighting you."

Stunned, Sam sat silently for a while, staring straight ahead. Suddenly, he said, "Let's call him. If he tries and flips this on us, we know he is gaslighting us. Or, at least me." They phoned Mike, who picked up and said, "Hey buddy. Are you okay now? You overreacted back there. I was worried about you."

"Did you tell my wife I was looking at other women and approached someone for her phone number?" Asked Sam, quietly. "What...I...What are you talking about? I never said that. Charl..." Mike spluttered before being interrupted by Charlene. "Mike, are you saying I am lying about you coming to my office two days ago to tell me that you were concerned about Sam looking at other women and that he even solicited a number from one of them?" Charlene asked. "Charlene...honey...you must have misunderstood what I said. I never said that. What I was trying to tell you is that you should be careful to take good care of my friend because there are many women out there who would want a man like that. Remember, I even told you I would get you proof of how many women want him?"

Charlene and Sam looked at each other silently, as Mike continued to lie. "Guys...guys...are you there? Look, this has been a huge misunderstanding. I can come over right now and we can clear it up. I am on my way over. I'll bring some wine we can hash this out and have a great night," said Mike.

"Don't come near me or my family ever again. If I see you or hear that you have come near my wife or my kids, I will get a restraining order against you." Mike started sobbing on the other side of the line. "Don't do this bro. We can sort this out. I have nothing but love for you and your kids. Charlene is lying, man. You will come back to me one day when she dumps you and takes your kids. I know, I know."

Sam replaced the phone and called his sons downstairs. "Trey, Tyler, we have to tell you something. Uncle Mike is not welcome here anymore and you are not to have anything to do with him. Okay?" "Sure Dad", said Trey. "I didn't trust him anyway. He told Tyler that you and mom were fighting so bad that he was here to make sure you guys didn't get a divorce. He asked Tyler to tell him everything that was going on at home, so he could help you guys. When Tyler told me, I told him it was a lie, but we were afraid to tell you because he was your friend."

It turned out, Mike's wife had left him and taken his two daughters with her because of his gaslighting behavior. He picked up the habit in college and used it on multiple women he dated and some of his friends.

Signs of a toxic friendship

It is very important to discern when a friendship has become toxic. In some cases, the friendship is toxic from the beginning and in other cases, it gradually becomes toxic over time. Signs that a friendship has become toxic include:

Putting you down

A toxic gaslighting friend is more concerned with being right and having control over you than your best interests. In a healthy friendship, the feedback you receive is positive and uplifting, even motivating you. Corrections are made out of love, not out of malice. In a toxic friendship, the "friend" will play on your insecurities and even reinforce them in order to dominate you.

Exerting control

Speaking of dominating you, a toxic friendship tips the scales of balance to favor one person. The toxic friend will dictate where you go, what you do, and even influence how you dress or speak to them. By exerting control over you, they effectively take away your power to make your own choices and give themselves control over these choices.

Blame

We all make mistakes, but when the controlling person makes the problem about you and tries to exonerate themselves, leaving you with the blame, you are in a toxic friendship. Toxic friends will not take responsibility for their actions if they have negative results. You will be blamed for even the slightest issue that arises when you are in their presence.

Emotional blackmail

This tactic involves withholding support or affection to the victim in circumstances where they need it. Toxic friends give their love conditionally and their love is only based on what you can give them. If you aren't available to them, they will not return your call, pick up your calls, or reply to your texts. They want to teach you a lesson by not being available to you.

Humiliation

Friends like to rib each other and teasing is a special part of friendship, but toxic friends take this to another level with deliberate humiliation. They will even laugh at the expense of the victim. If a friend constantly tells cruel jokes about you or laughs at your expense, they are abusing your friendship. If you have raised this as a concern with your friend and they tell you that you don't have a sense of humor, this is not a good friend.

Unpredictability

An inconsistency in your friend's personality that makes them unpredictable should be a red flag. If they are acting like this more often than not, they have the potential of creating a toxic environment for your friendship. In this type of friendship, you are never able to relax completely.

Common gaslighting phrases toxic friends say:

- You are being too sensitive.
- If you were a good friend, you would notice...
- I am like this with everyone, not just you,

- I was just kidding.
- You have no sense of humor.
- It's good to learn to laugh at yourself.
- What would you do without me?
- I can criticize you because we are friends.
- You know you are being insecure right now.
- It's no big deal.
- It's your fault our friendship isn't better.

CHAPTER EIGHT:

The Language and Culture of a Gaslighting Society

Gaslighting culture today

The culture we live in is very quick to judge anyone whose reality isn't in line with what they believe should be a reality. For example, in the Trump era, anyone who doesn't subscribe to "Making America Great Again" is ill-informed or worse. The liberals are the crazies, the conservatives are too uptight, and anyone in between doesn't have the backbone to back the "winning horse". Here are some ways the current American discourse has contributed to gaslighting culture:

Ignoring minorities

Gaslighting is more prevalent in today's culture because we have marginalized many people whose identities or practices don't fit in the narrow definition of what we have normalized in society. From the LGBTQ community to different religious groups, races, and political ideologies, we have opened up people to being gaslit by denying that their rights and freedoms are as important as those of others.

These denials have destabilized whole communities, which in turn destabilizes the entire nation. As a result, skewed leadership, like that of Donald Trump and Vladimir Putin, has gained a foothold and their lies and deceptions are now considered the truth.

Labeling people

The culture today is all about labels. You are either a failure or a success, depending on where you live, whom you live with, and how independent you are from your family. This has led to people losing support systems, like parents and siblings, because they want to appear successful. Inevitably, when they fall into the hands of gaslighters, they are easily isolated from their families, leaving them completely vulnerable. Such labels are used to measure the worth of a person, but they provide a foothold for nefarious emotional behavior.

Denying credit where it's due

The culture today is very accommodating of cultural appropriation without understanding that not only do the appropriators take credit for what they didn't create, they also deny the real creators their due credit. This practice leaves the communities who originally created the trend disempowered. It wipes out and trivializes the historical human trauma associated with slavery and colonization. By denying the culture and encouraging appropriation, you are gaslighting an entire community. This makes it easy to gaslight individuals from that community in a new, systematic form of oppression.

Rewiring the past

This means feeding the current generation lies about what happened in the past. The gaslighters will try to erase the historical injustices by tweaking the narrative to favor their own. For example, the rewiring of how black people organized sit-ins and safe spaces has had a direct impact on the reception of Colin Kapernick's peaceful kneeling protest against the killing of young black men. Add the rewiring to the words of gaslighters like President Donald Trump and society becomes desensitized to the past and now looks at the protest as the problem.

The future of gaslighting society

Gaslighting in the future is going to focus on our children and we are sending a signal to them that messing with another person's mental health is an acceptable way of interacting with them. Incidences of bullying, where the bully even encourages the victim to kill themselves, have been on the rise and the bully usually has narcissistic tendencies. They believe that they are somehow better than their victims.

To destabilize this nefarious trajectory in human interactions, we need to start having conversations with our kids about gaslighting, what happens when you are gaslit, how to avoid it, and overcome it in relationships and friendships.

In order to combat gaslighting, we need to demand better from our leaders and others around us. It must not be business as usual when the president lies or gaslights an individual.

Gaslighting and social media

Gaslighting in social media is known as cloutlighting. Social media has become a place of business and personal interactions, but it can also be a place where you find the most nefarious form of gaslighting. It gives the gaslighter a larger audience when discrediting their victim and may even attract other gaslighters to the gaslighting party, with the victim as the main target.

Take, for example, a group of friends with one who is a gaslighter. She will arrange events and exclude her gaslighting victim then post pictures of herself with the other friends on social media, knowing that the victim will see it. If the victim asks why she was excluded, the gaslighter makes her look bad in front of the other friends, effectively discrediting her. If she doesn't ask, she constantly wonders what she did wrong to be excluded from the event. In such a scenario, it is very easy for the gaslighter to rope in the other friends and make them accomplices in the gaslighting. Soon, the victim's distress becomes a source of entertainment for the rest of the group and they don't know what is going on behind the scenes with the victim and the gaslighter.

Cloutlighting involves the exploitation of the victim on social media to shock and even sometimes entertain others. Have you ever seen a video of a man or woman who seems to be overreacting to a seemingly normal situation and it seems funny at the expense of the person in the video? Imagine for a minute that the person is in an abusive relationship and has just been gaslit. The abuser records him or her and posts it online. You have just seen a victim of cloutlighting. The abuser is looking for sympathy from viewers of the video and also to paint the victim in a poor light. Your nasty comment about the victim is used by the abuser to reinforce the emotional abuse currently taking place.

Familiar everyday phrases people use to gaslight others:

- You take things too personally.
- You can't take a joke.
- You are too sensitive.
- We talked about this, can't you remember?
- I have to repeat myself?
- Don't you think you are overreacting?
- You like to jump to the wrong conclusion.
- Can you hear yourself?
- Stop taking things so seriously.
- Why are you upset about a joke?

Harmful phrases that vicious gaslighters use to disarm people:

You are imagining things.

This phrase is supposed to make you doubt your perception of what you experienced. Once you start to doubt yourself, the gaslighter starts to take control.

It was a joke.

Using this phrase makes you look and feel like you are deficient in humor and you need to not read into what the gaslighter says. Even though the gaslighter says you should take the joke at face value, they actually want you to internalize the meaning of the joke and start doubting yourself.

You are always overreacting. You are too sensitive.

This phrase makes it look like your reaction to the gaslighter is flawed. The correct reaction is what they are asking of you, which is not to be too sensitive.

You need to lighten up or let this go

This is a very dismissive phrase that is supposed to trivialize your feelings and make them unimportant. It is used in public to devalue your worth in social circles.

You are crazy

This phrase is popular because it sets the victim up as unstable and gains sympathy for the abuser at the same time.

CHAPTER NINE:

The Long-Term Effects of Gaslighting

How victims feel and their state of mind during the process of gaslighting

The simple truth behind the way the victim of gaslighting feels is a loss of value. They tend to feel completely devalued and unworthy of their abuser, which is exactly what he or she wants them to feel. The state-of-mind cycle of a victim of gaslighting, as it happens, include:

Disbelief

The victim usually can't believe the shift in the abuser. They begin to feel they have to do more to restore the healthy balance that was there before. The very first time the gaslighting begins, they will make excuses for the abuser, believing that it's just a bump in the relationship.

Defense

The more the abuser comes down at the victim, the more he or she tries to break them, but in the beginning, there is still some fight left in the victim. They will push back at this point because the gaslighting hasn't completely overtaken them.

Depression

This stage quickly follows the defense stage because the victim may feel like she or he is not able to withstand the abuse and constant put-downs. At this stage, it feels like they are constantly doing things wrong and there is an unhappy environment in their personal space all the time, so they gradually sink into depression.

Coming out of depression is hard and this is the stage where the gaslighter begins to win. At this point, the abuser can't afford to let up their psychological torment, so they will isolate the person in order to have unchallenged access to them.

General effects and deep impact of gaslighting

There are several general effects of gaslighting to look out for in yourself or your loved one if you suspect gaslighting:

Second-guessing

Second-guessing is a direct result of eroded confidence since the abuser makes the victim feel like their judgment is flawed about everything. They constantly ask themselves if what they saw was real, or if they made the right decision.

Fear

There is a general aura of fear surrounding the victim of gaslighting. They are constantly afraid to make the abuser upset, afraid they will lose everything, afraid no one will believe them, and afraid to start all over again.

Constantly apologizing

The abuser always has the victim in defensive mode, so they are constantly sorry for their "flaws" which are breaking down the relationship. The victim can even begin to apologize for their existence, which means they are very delicate mentally and could harm themselves.

Depression

It is common for victims of gaslighting to become depressed and melancholy. Nothing rouses them from their fog of sadness and they constantly accept the abuse and put-downs from the gaslighter as their deserved reward.

Withholding information

Victims are usually conditioned to withhold information because the abuser tries to turn everyone against them. If they do not find support in the first person they tell, they may not ever feel like they can tell anyone else. Plus, there is a lot of shame still associated with all forms of abuse and the victims are usually the ones who feel the most ashamed.

Indecision

The victim will grapple with even the simplest decisions and look for someone to make them for him or her. This is because of their co-dependency on the abuser to make every decision. If he or she is not in the picture, they can become completely incapacitated in making the most basic decision.

Guilt

Some victims feel guilty talking about how bad their abuser is when he has been so good in the past. Friends and family may feel like they are being ungrateful or are gold diggers.

Emotional trauma and symptoms

It is important to recognize that victims of gaslighting have been traumatized in such deep ways that it will take years to undo the damage if it can even be undone. The majority of victims exhibit these trauma symptoms, which may be countered in time if identified early enough:

- Hypervigilance (anticipation of additional trauma).
- Flashbacks of painful events, which occur at any time of day or night.
- Heightened anxiety.
- Unpredictable mood swings.
- Mental confusion.
- Intrusive memories.

These are core symptoms that have taken years to develop and may be managed, but never really go away.

Cognitive dissonance

Like I said earlier, cognitive dissonance is the state of mind where one holds two different beliefs and one goes against the other, due to psychological stress. For victims of gaslighting, they believe that their very survival is dependent on their abuser and it is acceptable for the gaslighter to behave as he or she does. The anger and hate shown by the abuser are because he or she loves them and is protecting them against themselves.

For example, a woman in an abusive relationship hates the pain and abuse, but she is even more afraid of what she will face without him. After all, he loves her. They are willing to die rather than face life without the abuser, so they will defend his behavior from family and friends. In gaslighting, the victim tries to mute their cognitive dissonance to survive the internal conflict they feel. This helps them manage their primitive anxiety arising from the situation they find themselves in.

Unfortunately, during this time, they convince themselves that things are not that bad and when the abuser shows them some kindness, they believe things will get better. For victims of gaslighting, cognitive dissonance becomes a crutch they lean on to survive their hell.

How gaslighting in toxic relationships works to erode reality and sense of self

The gaslighter is always one step ahead of their victim in their game, meaning they have already planned ahead using these three steps to erode the reality and sense of self of their victim:

The idealization stage

In this stage, the gaslighter puts their best foot forward, effectively manipulating the victim into trusting them. The victim can do no wrong according to the narcissist, who will lavish them with attention and affection. This deludes the victim into believing she or he is in a loving relationship and makes them let down their guard.

The devaluation stage

During this stage, the gaslighter becomes cold and calculating towards the victim. She or he can do nothing right and is constantly showered with criticism in place of love. This launches the victim into depression and they increasingly try to make their abuser happy, with no success. They begin to feel unworthy and like a failure. This stage is extremely devastating because it can easily chart the pattern of future relationships.

The discarding stage

This is the period during which the abuser figures out how to discard the victim. They may walk out on them, have them committed for mental instability, or even have them killed. The most important thing is getting rid of them. The more the victim tries to hold on to the relationship, the more powerful and even crueler the abuser becomes. The gaslighter will always dangle the possibility of discarding their victim to make him or her cling on even more.

CHAPTER TEN:

Proof of Gaslighting

Common gaslighting techniques you should know for when it hits you

Lies and denial

The one thing we have fully established is that a gaslighter is a liar. They will lie blatantly about anything and everything. The pattern of lies is used to condition their victim and establish themselves as his or her point of authority.

Projection

Gaslighting is characterized by the abuser projecting their own failings and insecurities onto the victim. If they are sloppy, they will blame the victim for being sloppy. If they struggle with keeping time, they will blame the victim for being constantly late when he or she is two minutes late. If they are cheating, they will accuse their victim of cheating to cover their actions.

Diverting

The gaslighter will divert the conversation by changing the entire subject and refusing to acknowledge the concerns of their victim. Sometimes, they will completely refuse to listen or respond to issues the victim raises.

Incongruence

This means that they don't mean what they say. The words coming from a gaslighter can be mismatched to their actions. They will say I love you, followed with unloving actions, like the silent treatment and cold looks or sulking.

Countering

Challenging the victim's memories and reality is a game to the gaslighter and they will play the game for as long as you are together. They love how you have to rely on them for information.

Isolation

When you notice your potential partner trying to drive a wedge between you and your loved ones, it is time to ask yourself why. Isolation is the key to effective gaslighting because it leaves the victim vulnerable to attack from the abuser without any support system.

The 5 steps of gaslighters: Learn how they do it

1. They use your fear against you

You have let the gaslighter in and they are now close to you and trusted. You confide in them and, instead of protecting you, they use your fears against you. For example, for the longest time, Americans have railed on and on about the deep state and the Washington swamp. Donald Trump has used these fears and concerns to gaslight the American people and every time he is taken to task, he says the deep state is after him because he is working for the Americans.

2. They act as if they know more about you than anyone

Every time you have an argument with a gaslighter, they will use something negative about your shortcomings against you. For example, if you are not good with finances, they will say, "You know I know you better than anyone. You can't manage money. You are horrible at finances. That is why I am here to take care of stuff like that."

3. They normalize disrespect

During the stage where the abuser is trying to devalue the victim, he will normalize the disrespect every time she calls him out on it. For example, the man will say things like, "Can you hear yourself? You sound crazy." And the woman pushes back with, "Hey don't call me crazy." "Baby, learn to take a joke. I was just kidding," replies the man. Soon enough, he will be calling her crazy and she will accept it because he is just joking and she is being sensitive.

4. They question your commitment

By questioning your commitment, they are casting aspersions on the stability of the relationship. For example, they will demand something they know you can't do, like spend all your savings on their project, and when you don't, they become extremely sad and even threaten to end it or harm themselves.

5. They invest in negative affirmations

They make you doubt yourself by using negative statements as absolute truths about you. For example, the abuser will tell their victim, "I don't know how they haven't fired you from this job. You can barely handle your workload. You don't have what it takes."

Simple responses to smoke a gaslighter that gets them every time

Use the stare

Look at the person who made the comment for a long while, taking in their reaction. The uncomfortable mounting silence is usually enough to launch them into an apology or make them embarrassed. Try it and see the shame come over your would-be gaslighter. The stare is a great way to express disbelief in what the gaslighter is saying, every time you doubt their story.

Remember each mistake

A gaslighter is meticulous in remembering their victim's mistake, so make sure you remember theirs. If they slip up on a story they told you, make sure you call them out on it.

Intentionally misunderstand them

You can see the gaslighter is trying to feed you a bogus narrative and lie blatantly to you. Don't allow yourself to be swayed. Instead, act like you don't understand. For example, say something like, "I can't understand how we saw the same thing and you and I have different versions of it. Interesting how the human brain works. I know what I saw and I am sure you know what you saw. I can't change your mind and neither can you change mine. Let's just agree to disagree."

Do some countering of your own

You said you flushed the toilet and he says you didn't. But you were recording yourself singing as you use the loo. Provide the evidence and counter his or her lies. If he says he texted you to cancel plans and you know he didn't, ask him to show you the text. This lets him know you are on to his game. If something matters to you and the gaslighter tries to trivialize it, call him or her out on it immediately.

Quick comebacks for gaslighting scripts

Gaslighter: "I didn't say that."
Comeback: "You did and from now on I will start recording our conversations, so you can't deny your own words."

Gaslighter: "I look forward to dinner this Friday. Thanks for the invite."

Comeback: "I didn't invite you to dinner. I told you I have a soul cycle class with my friends."

Gaslighter: "I never confirmed that date"
Comeback: "Yes, you did. Here is your text confirming the date."

Gaslighter: "But you said you would help me pay for this stuff. How am I supposed to pay for it?"
Comeback: "I don't know. I never said I would help you pay for your clothes. I told you I may have some money and if I can, I will. This is not my responsibility."

Gaslighter: "Don't be so sensitive."
Comeback: "That is disrespectful. I don't tell you how to feel or act, so don't tell me how to feel."

Gaslighter: "Can't you take a joke?"
Comeback: "What was funny about this? Is it the part where you made fun of me in public or you told everyone my personal business?"

Gaslighter: "I texted you to cancel the date. Didn't you see my text?"
Comeback: "No, I didn't see any message. Show me the text."

Gaslighter: "You don't love me like I love you."
Comeback: "Look, I can only love you like I know how to love you. You do not set the standard of how to love."

Simple ideas to fight the effects of gaslighting

Confront

Do not let the gaslighter back you into submission when you know he or she is lying. It will definitely anger the abuser to see you push back, but it also tells them that you are no pushover. Take a minute and compose yourself, so you are very clear about what you are confronting.

The responsive tactic will be to placate you and make you feel like you are overreacting.

Ask for an explanation

The gaslighter cannot explain their actions when asked to because they understand their nefarious nature. This puts them on the defensive and the responsive tactic is usually to get emotional and accuse you of not loving them or to blame you for a misunderstanding.

Prove yourself

If the gaslighter says you are not good at something and that is why they need to be there for you, point out instances where you have done that particular task well and excelled. It becomes harder for the gaslighter to criticize with no proof. And if they still want to argue, refuse, citing your proof.

Demand respect

The gaslighter will test your limits in terms of respect. Demand respect and end the relationship if none is forthcoming. Do not give the gaslighter a chance to become disrespectful because it will only go downhill from here.

A new skill to combat gaslighting

Mindfulness

Mindfulness is our basic human ability to stay in the present and be aware of our surroundings and our actions. The gaslighter will strive to alter your reality, but mindfulness will keep you in the present, able to counter any false narratives that they may try to spin.

Mindfulness gives you the confidence and ammunition to confront any situation. To cultivate mindfulness, you need to:

Build your gut instinct

Your gut instinct will never steer you wrong. Call it intuition if you will, but it tells you if a situation doesn't feel right. Gaslighting is based on lies, so trust your gut instinct if it tells you that you are being lied to.

Keep a journal

A gaslighter is an ever-changing animal, so keeping a journal that tells you what they said and when they said it and it will help you keep track of the facts. You may need to keep a journal in secret.

Meditate

The gaslighter likes to overpower you by calling you names and using put-downs to manipulate your mental health. Meditate and protect your mindfulness. Not only does this relax you, but it also gives you clarity.

Exercise

Easier said than done, but exercise will put your mind and body in sync. A healthy body and mind are harder for a gaslighter to control. The stress and PTSD from being around a gaslighter can be countered by taking some time to do yoga or Tai Chi.

FINAL WORDS

This book is meant to help you recognize and combat gaslighting before it takes root and has debilitating effects on yourself or your loved one. Gaslighting is a common occurrence that has gained momentum as a form of abuse and has been used for a long time to gain control over the victim. For some people, using gaslighting is a conscious decision, but there are some gaslighters who don't know that they are indulging in this behavior.

I've talked about gaslighting in the context of intimate relationships, family units, workplaces, and friendships. You should now be able to understand the approach of the gaslighter and what they want from their victim. I've also shed some light on how you can identify gaslighting in your life in any context.

The gaslighter personality is fraught with insecurities, fears, doubts, low self-worth, and low self-esteem. These character issues play a huge role in making the gaslighter a controlling, manipulative individual. Whether you are dealing with an aware or unaware gaslighter, the effect on the victim is the same.

It is crucial to know what type of gaslighter you're dealing with in order to be able to effectively see their patterns. The minute one becomes abusive and threatens you, this is an Intimidator Gaslighter. If you are dealing with a Jekyll and Hyde type of gaslighter, he or she fits the profile of a Good Guy Gaslighter. This type of gaslighter is perhaps the most insidious of all. The Glamour Gaslighter can be identified by his or her thoroughbred behavior, which they use to entrance you and eventually cause you to be beholden to them.

Self-examination is crucial in a relationship because you may be exhibiting gaslighting behavior, unknowingly. Some of the questions I've outlined can be instrumental in helping you identify if you are on the gaslighting spectrum and, if you are, how extreme are you? This book effectively helps you to understand all of the above and recognize the patterns.

The promise I made in this book was to give you all the information I could about gaslighting, to lay bare its intentions, and cite examples doing so. Using the examples and stories in the book, you can now identify gaslighting in your life and the lives of those around you and you can find a solution.

The biggest takeaway from this book should be that the victim of gaslighting is not at fault. You are dealing with an expert manipulator who has no scruples and doesn't play fair. Many victims show resilience and they are to be admired for their fighting spirit because a gaslighter doesn't go down without a fight. If you know someone who is being gaslit, remain as the constant in their lives, a safe haven for them, and always watch over them.

EXCLUSIVE GIFT

Hello! Thank you for purchasing this book. Here is your free gift. It's good and it's free!

This mini e-book will answer your questions about this rather controversial skill. It's controversial because it works!

Get ready to learn more about Conversational Hypnosis, simplified for easy and practical use.

Here are just a few of the many benefits of learning Conversational Hypnosis:

- Get your audience to warm up to you and be more open to your message
- Better sales tactics
- Create deeper connections with people
- Create positive change
- And more!

If you want to become a good hypnotic conversationalist, you better start learning the skill today and be a master tomorrow. All you have to do is access the secret download page below.

Open a browser window on your computer or smartphone and enter: <u>bonus.emorygreen.com</u>

You will be automatically directed to the download page.

Remember to influence the world with good intentions.

All the best,
Emory Green

Printed in Great Britain
by Amazon

68487429R00068